The

Female Diplomat

Stories of Strength, Silence, and the Unseen World of Women Who Carry Nations in Their Hearts.

Oluwakemi Amuda

Advance Praise

The following reflections are offered by senior ambassadors and diplomats who reviewed the manuscript and affirmed its depth, clarity, and contribution to the global diplomatic discourse.

"This book, by a female scholar-diplomat, makes huge contributions to the academic study of international relations and to members of the diplomatic community. It provides real linkages between theory and practice at both the bilateral and multilateral levels of diplomatic engagement. The book would also be of great value to the general readership interested in the dynamics of peaceful resolutions of violent conflicts in an increasingly turbulent international system." - **Ambassador Prof. Ibrahim Agboola GAMBARI. – Fmr. Chief of Staff to Nigeria President**

"The Female Diplomat stands as a work of rare composure and intellectual grace, an enduring testament to courage practiced in silence, leadership exercised with restraint, and institutions that demand strength without spectacle. It dignifies service and elevates the unseen labour of diplomacy." - **Ambassador Hussein Abdullahi - Fmr. Under. Secretary. (MFA)**

"This book is a tour de force that provides an account of the lived experiences of female diplomats, which will serve as a lesson and a guide for young female officers who want to build a career in the foreign service globally." - **Ambassador Abubakar Jidda – Consul General of Nigeria, New York**

Advance Praise

"The Female Diplomat is an outstanding publication that gives voice to a perspective too often overrepresented in global conversations. It is not just a book; it is a window into the strength, intelligence, and quiet resilience that women bring to diplomacy and leadership." - **Amb. (Prof) Olufolake Abdulrasaq – Kwara State First Lady.**

"The book offers an engaging and realistic portrayal of women in diplomacy, blending lived experience with insightful reflection. It highlights the resilience and adaptability required to navigate both professional and social spaces, making it an inspiring read for current and aspiring female diplomats globally." - **Ambassador Agnes Chimbiri-Molande – Perm, Representative of the Republic of Malawi to the United Nations**

"The Female Diplomat is not just a book; it is a mirror, a testimony, and a legacy for the next generation of diplomatic leaders." A profound and necessary work." – **Prof. Ugoji Adanma. Eze Esq. PhD**

"This book captures the emotional, intellectual, and institutional realities of diplomatic life with rare honesty and elegance" – **Professor Dr. Xian Smcihang- Global Affairs Analyst**

Copyright Page

The Female Diplomat

Manhattan/New York

ISBN (Paperback): 979-8-0056458-6-3

ISBN (Hardcover): 979-8-0056458-7-0

ISBN (eBook):

First Edition, 2026

Printed in the United States of America.

Dedication

To every woman who has carried a nation in one hand

and her private world in the other.
To the ones who stood alone, who spoke when silence was easier,

who endured what the world will never fully understand.
And to God, whose guidance steadied my steps and

whose breath animated every page.

Her strength is not in the volume of her voice, but in the steadiness of her presence." - Kemi.

Preface

The Female Diplomat originated from a persistent inquiry that followed me through every posting and every corridor of service: **Who represents the women who speak for nations?** I wrote this book because their narratives are too often quietened, their struggles diminished or overlooked, and their bravery mistaken for routine. The global community benefits from their labour, yet rarely pauses to recognise the weight of their burdens or the resilience required to remain composed in environments never originally designed for them.

This work stands as an homage to the esteemed profession that sustains global understanding, and to the international community that depends on the discreet, persistent efforts of those who negotiate, interpret, and protect fragile diplomatic spaces. Above all, it celebrates the women who have upheld their integrity in the world's most sensitive moments, standing firm not because it was easy, but because the circumstances demanded such resolve. It is also a reflection for future generations: a mirror through which they may see themselves clearly, acknowledge their strengths, and step confidently into spaces once deemed inaccessible, assured that they rightfully belong. In this context.

The Female Diplomat is more than a book. It is a record of existence. A testament to resilience. A declaration that the women who bear the burdens of nations deserve recognition, acknowledgement, and remembrance. The Female Diplomat does not seek to ignite controversy or unveil protected knowledge. It preserves the sanctity of institutional confidentiality, offering insight without revealing any information that could endanger individuals, missions, institutions, or nations.

Table of Contents

Note on Text

This publication is based on genuine diplomatic experiences amassed through extensive service across various continents, cultures, and political landscapes. While the reflections and narratives are rooted in personal experience, they are deliberately structured to safeguard confidentiality, protect institutional integrity, and uphold the dignity of all referenced individuals. Certain characters are composite representations, designed to shield identities while retaining the emotional and intellectual essence of the encounters that inspired them. Events have been reorganised, anonymised, or rephrased where appropriate, without compromising the authenticity of the lessons conveyed.

The philosophical and diplomatic insights presented herein are derived from a synthesis of practice, observation, and scholarly inquiry. They reflect the author's engagement with global governance, leadership theory, political psychology, gender studies, and the spiritual dimensions of public service. Cultural references are handled with respect and contextual awareness, acknowledging the intricacy of depicting diverse societies within a unified narrative framework.

This section aims to clarify the methodological decisions that have influenced the manuscript, thereby ensuring transparency for readers, scholars, and practitioners who may utilise this work for research, reflection, or professional development. The integrity of the truth remains intact, even where the details have been ethically adapted. *The female Diplomat seeks to preserve the sacred boundaries of diplomatic confidentiality while illuminating the human experience behind the role. Every narrative is crafted with respect for the sanctity of diplomatic confidentiality and the integrity of the offices I have served.*

Author's Note

This book is not a biography, nor is it a technical guide to diplomacy. It is a testament to the emotional labour, intellectual discipline, and quiet spiritual resilience that shape the life of the female diplomat. The reflections and narratives within these pages arise from lived personal experiences, formed in negotiation rooms, along the corridors of missions and ministries, and in the private spaces where women gather themselves after carrying the burdens of national representation.

Certain names, timelines, and contextual details have been adjusted to preserve confidentiality, yet the essence of the truth remains preserved. What you will encounter here is not a chronological account of events, but the inner architecture of a distinguished profession often defined by discretion, complexity, and unseen sacrifice.

This work offers a window into the emotional and spiritual terrain of women who serve, the weight they carry, the silences they navigate, and the strength they cultivate to stand with clarity and integrity in the world. It is both a reflection and a record: a formal acknowledgement of a diplomat's reality, and a personal offering to those who have lived it, are living it, or will one day walk this path.

Introduction

Diplomacy is often described using technical terminology, such as negotiation, statecraft, the management of interests, and the architecture of the international order. Nonetheless, for the female diplomat, diplomacy encompasses more than mere professional obligations; it also involves navigating intricate social terrain. Her daily experience is shaped by her identity, perceptions, emotional landscapes, and the subtle balance between visibility and vulnerability. She must sustain a discreet yet impactful presence, demonstrate firmness without being perceived as difficult, exhibit brilliance without incurring accusations of ambition, and display human qualities without seeming weak.

Her work unfolds across two parallel spheres: the international stage and her inner personal landscape. She bears the expectations of her nation while simultaneously managing the unspoken societal expectations imposed upon her as a woman.

She negotiates treaties and manages crises while engaging in self-negotiation, articulating her voice, defining her boundaries, preserving her dignity, and advancing her personal development. Each environment she enters demands a meticulous calibration of her presence. Every decision she makes is scrutinised through the lenses of cultural, political, and gendered influences. Yet she remains resilient.

She dedicates herself to service.

She demonstrates excellence.

This book invites the reader into that inner world, the realm behind the protocol, the polished statements, and the diplomatic smile that must remain steady even as the ground beneath her shifts. It is a world shaped by power and silence, resilience and restraint, intuition and intellect. It is a world in which emotional labour is not an accessory to the job but a core instrument of statecraft.

It is a world where female diplomats must learn to lead not only with skill but also with a profound self-awareness that constitutes their subtle authority. *"The Female Diplomat"* examines the complexities of this existence: the burden of representation, the sacrifice of invisibility, the discipline of maintaining composure, the courage to speak when silence is expected, and the prudence to refrain from speaking when it might be misinterpreted. It explores the delicate negotiations she undertakes internally long before engaging in any formal gathering. The work pays tribute to the resilience necessary to uphold integrity within a profession that often necessitates fragmentation.

This book does not advocate sympathy; rather, it advocates recognition. It stands as a testament to women who have borne nations on their shoulders while preserving their humanity with grace. It documents their endurance, brilliance, sacrifices, and unacknowledged victories. It serves as a reminder that diplomacy is not merely an art of managing international affairs; it is also an art of self-management within the global context.

Reading this book entails immersing oneself in the life of a woman positioned at the confluence of history and expectation, service and selfhood. It offers insight into the emergence of a leader who has mastered the art of converting pressure into clarity, silence into strategy, and resilience into a lasting legacy. This is her story.
Told with reverence.
Told with truth.
Told at last

PART I

FOUNDATIONS OF DIPLOMATIC IDENTITY

"Her presence is quiet, yet it steadies the room before words are spoken." - Kemi.

Architectural Prelude

Before delivering her inaugural speech at an international forum, a female diplomat is inherently influenced by historical and extensive factors. Part I of this publication examines the subtle structures that underpin every diplomatic career, including the systems, hierarchies, expectations, and emotional dimensions that shape the professional identity of female diplomats.

This chapter delineates the formative moments that shape her: the moment she enters the diplomatic sphere, the subtle negotiations of presence, the unspoken conventions she must understand, and the intangible burdens she must bear before participating in diplomatic deliberations.

This section elucidates the diplomat's development not through titles or assignments but through the internal calibrations she undertakes as she acquires the skills to navigate a world not intrinsically designed for her. It is here that she uncovers the politics of visibility, the toll of being underestimated, and the quiet bravery required to articulate truth in rooms that scrutinise her before extending trust.

Part I discusses her convergence, the development of her voice, stance, authority, and self-perception within the institution. It provides the foundation for all subsequent progress.

CHAPTER ONE

Constructing the Diplomatic Self: Gender, Identity, and State Representation

The Weight of Representation

Identity in diplomacy is not a static possession; it is an evolving architecture shaped by gender, state power, and institutional expectations. A diplomat does not merely represent her nation; she becomes the living embodiment of its narrative, contradictions, and aspirations. For the female diplomat, this embodiment carries added weight: she represents a state that has not always represented her. Her presence in diplomatic space is therefore both an act of service and an act of becoming. She must construct herself within an institution that predates her, defines her, and often misinterprets her before she speaks.

From the moment she enters the foreign service, she assumes a role within a framework not originally intended for her. Nevertheless, she must do so with authority. She learns the nuanced art of representation, the subtle negotiations among her personal identity, the institution's expectations, and the perceptions of the external world. Her identity becomes layered and dynamic, influenced by her inherent self, the self dictated by the institution, the self interpreted by others, and the self she must safeguard to maintain her integrity. These layers do not always align; at times, they conflict, fracture, or coalesce into coherence through conscious internal effort. This marks the inception of the diplomatic self.

A Room That Tests Her

Helsinki greeted her with a cold so clean it felt like truth.

Minister Counsellor Amara Nwosu, representing Nigeria, entered the negotiation hall aware of the stakes before her.

A regional security agreement, developed over several months, was now endangered by an abrupt political realignment. The chamber was occupied by senior officials, predominantly older men, their voices conveying the impatience typical of those accustomed to exerting control. The Political Section had provided her with thorough preparation; however, the atmosphere revealed a deeper truth: preparation alone does not eliminate gendered expectations. Her authority would be challenged before her competence was fully recognised.

When the discussion turned tense, a delegate pointed at her and said, “Your country must decide now. We don’t have time for hesitation.” The provocation was intentional.

The pressure was calculated.

The expectation was clear: react, defend, or retreat.

But Amara did none of these.

She inhaled once, slowly and deliberately, drawing on years of training to maintain composure under pressure. Subsequently, she articulated her thoughts with a calmness that conveyed greater authority than mere volume.

“A rushed decision is a broken agreement,” she stated. “Let us proceed with clarity, not haste."

Her restraint was not passive; rather, it was a calculated strategy. She declined to be swayed by artificial urgency. She refused to allow the room to dictate her pace. She abstained from performing the expected reaction.

The atmosphere shift.

The tension eased.

The negotiation recalibrated.

The chairperson paused, nodded, and then redirected the discussion. The delegation that had previously attempted to corner her reduced its pressure.

The entire room aligned with her lead, not because of an explicit demand, but because she imparted stability through a disciplined presence. By the conclusion of the meeting, the agreement had been strengthened, the project timeline revised, and a joint technical working group formally established.

The Ministry subsequently acknowledged that her intervention averted a premature collapse of the negotiations. No one offered applause or extended gratitude to her. Nonetheless, all participants adapted their approaches in response to her.

Influence often does not manifest overtly; at times, it simply reorients the collective environment.

The Paradox of Being Seen Before Being Heard

Amara's experience reveals a deeper truth about diplomatic identity: representation is not the projection of identity; it is the negotiation of it.

Gender is not a variable; it is a structural condition that shapes how a person is seen before speaking, and legitimacy is not granted; it is constructed through clarity, preparation, and disciplined presence.

Amara's physical presence precedes her voice as she enters the room. Her gender is a subject of interpretive discourse well before she articulates herself, leading to her being perceived as a symbol, anomaly, threat, or token, seldom as neutral. Neutrality remains a privilege reserved for individuals whose identities conform to institutional standards.

Thus, the construction of the diplomatic self begins with a paradox: she must represent a state that has not fully represented her. This paradox shapes her early years in service, as she quickly learns that diplomacy is not only about treaties and negotiations; it is about managing perceptions, navigating assumptions, and performing legitimacy in rooms where her authority is questioned before she speaks.

The Dual Consciousness of the Female Diplomat

Her courage is not loud. It is the kind that holds a room steady without raising her voice. Her strength is built on intangible moments: late nights preparing briefs, internal debates before speaking, emotional labour in culturally demanding settings, and the tension between family and country.

These moments forge a dual consciousness, the professional self she must perform and the gendered reality she must navigate. This duality does not weaken her; it sharpens her. It becomes the foundation of her diplomatic identity.

To understand the female diplomat is to recognise a courage that is both subtle and formidable. It is the courage to serve with distinction in environments that challenge her presence, to lead with empathy in systems that reward assertiveness, to maintain authenticity in settings that demand conformity, and to steady a room without dominating it. Her courage is not decorative; it is structural. Her presence is not symbolic; it is transformative. Her identity is not accidental; it is engineered.

Lessons Learned: Diplomatic Identity in Practice

Amara's experience in Helsinki demonstrates that the diplomatic self is not innate; rather, it is cultivated through intentional internal effort. She discovers that urgency often serves as a strategic illusion rather than an objective reality, and that resisting it requires clarity, courage, and emotional discipline.

Her composed intervention illustrates that authority need not be vocal to be impactful; understated power can influence a room more decisively than overt force.

She also discovers that gender is not merely a footnote in the realm of diplomacy; rather, it is a fundamental structural condition that shapes perception well before competence assessments are conducted. Her identity precedes her voice upon entering a room, necessitating her to navigate assumptions, manage interpretations, and safeguard aspects of herself that the institution is unable to contain. Solitude serves as a crucible in which her conviction is tempered, imparting to her that effective leadership often entails steadfastness in the absence of external affirmation.

Lessons Learned in Representation

Most importantly, she recognises that representation is not merely performance but a process of negotiation, involving an ongoing balancing act among the self she presents, the self the institution demands, the self that others interpret, and the self she must maintain to preserve her integrity.

These insights constitute the foundational elements of her diplomatic identity, illustrating that the courage of a female diplomat is not superficial but fundamental. It embodies a quiet, disciplined strength that stabilises a room, influences outcomes, and broadens the scope of leadership without raising one's voice.

CHAPTER TWO

When Truth Enters the Institution: Navigating Early Diplomatic Realities

The Nature of Quiet Courage

Courage is often imagined as something loud, manifesting through forceful declarations or dramatic interventions. However, in the realm of diplomacy, courage often manifests differently. It is characterised by quietness, deliberation, and internal strength. It observes before speaking, discerns before acting, and emerges only when the situation demands it.

This embodies the silent courage of the female diplomat: the juncture at which truth, moulded by lived experience and tempered with restraint, ultimately integrates into the institution.

The bravery exhibited by a female diplomat is fostered well before she enters a negotiation chamber. It originates from the private resolve to persevere in a realm that questions her presence, challenges her authority, and underestimates her resilience. It manifests in the early hours as she prepares to serve a nation that may never fully comprehend the emotional and personal sacrifices inherent in her duties. It is evident in instances when she chooses dignity over reactive tendencies, clarity over hostility, and composure over the impulse to retreat.

Her courage is not impetuous; rather, it is grounded in the discipline of self-awareness and understanding of her responsibilities.

A Room Charged with Assumptions

Brussels received her with polite distance, the kind that tests before it trusts.

Ambassador Selam Tesfaye of Ethiopia arrived for a multilateral meeting months in the making. The Political Section had briefed her thoroughly: the agenda centred on a regional development framework requiring consensus among states with competing priorities. The atmosphere in the Belgian capital was tense; recent political shifts had unsettled the coalition, and several delegations had adopted increasingly defensive postures. The room she entered was not neutral. It was charged with the subtle hierarchies and unspoken assumptions that shape diplomatic space.

Inside the meeting hall, delegates exchanged sharp remarks, each defending national interests with practised precision. Selam presented a proposal grounded in three years of fieldwork, regional consultations, and direct engagement with affected communities. It was substantive, evidence-based, and aligned with the working groups' technical recommendations.

Yet a senior delegate dismissed her contribution with a casual wave of his hand.

"Let's hear from someone with more experience," he said.

The room shifted.

Eyes darted.

Silence thickened.

The dismissal was not about her proposal; it was about her presence. It was not a critique of her ideas; it was a negation of her legitimacy.

When Truth Refuses to Shrink

Selam felt the familiar sting, not of insult, but of recognition.

She had been here before.

Many women had. She inhaled slowly, letting the moment settle. Then she spoke with a calm that carried more authority than volume.

"With respect, Ambassador," she said, "the proposal you dismissed is the culmination of three years of fieldwork, regional consultations, and direct engagement with the affected communities. I will articulate my truth, because no one else in this room has lived the realities that informed this work."

In that moment, truth entered the institution.

The room stilled. Not because she raised her voice, but because she refused to shrink. Not because she demanded space, but because she occupied it fully, as someone who had earned it. Her intervention shifted the atmosphere. Delegates who had been silent leaned forward. The chair requested a technical review of her proposal. The Secretariat acknowledged the need to incorporate her findings. The working group reconvened with renewed seriousness.

By the end of the session, her proposal, once dismissed, had become the foundation of the revised framework. A joint task team was established to operationalise its recommendations. The meeting communiqué reflected her language on community engagement and regional equity.

No one congratulated her.

No one admitted they had been wrong. But the institution moved in the direction she set.

The Weight of Being the Counterargument

This passage explores the significant nexus between truth and institutional influence: it highlights the bravery required to remain resolute in environments that aim to suppress her; the bravery to articulate when silence is anticipated; the bravery to stand firm without succumbing to insensitivity; and the bravery to lead without emulating the prevailing leadership style in the room.

Selam's bravery was not loud.

It was rooted in competence, preparation, and the knowledge that she belonged, even when others forgot. Her presence became the counterargument. Her steadiness became the recalibration. Her truth became the shift.

Quiet courage is the enduring strength to persist when society presumes she should be grateful merely for being included. It is the resilience required to navigate cultures that misinterpret her confidence as arrogance, her calm as weakness, and her firmness as defiance. It is the wisdom to know when to assert, when to pause, and when to let presence speak more powerfully than words.

The Unseen Courage Behind the Role

Her courage extends beyond external challenges; it reaches her inner world. It takes courage to leave family behind for postings across continents; to rebuild her life every few years in unfamiliar cities; to carry the emotional weight of crises while tending to the emotional needs of loved ones; to remain resilient in public while being vulnerable in private; to succeed in a profession not designed with her in mind, yet to rise above its challenges.

The female diplomat does not wear her courage like armour. She bears it as fundamentally as breath, constant, silent, and vital. Her courage is not shown through dramatic gestures; it resides in the steadfastness of the space she refuses to relinquish. It is not measured by the battles she fights but by the dignity with which she holds her ground. It is not reflected in external recognition but demonstrated through perseverance in moments when no one is watching.

This is the essence of truth entering the institution: a courage that stabilises nations, shapes decisions, and sustains global cohesion in ways seldom recorded in history books.

Lessons Learned: Truth as Diplomatic Influence

Selam's experience in Brussels reveals that truth must be articulated with precision, not volume. Institutions respond to clarity, even when they resist it, and dismissal is often a test, not a verdict. Influence does not always announce itself; sometimes it simply reorients the room.

Her three years of fieldwork became her legitimacy. Preparation became a form of power. Institutions eventually recognise what is undeniable; Substance, when delivered with steadiness, becomes difficult to ignore. Leadership is not always acknowledged, but it is always felt.

Most importantly, she learns that when truth enters the institution through the voice of a female diplomat, it does not arrive with spectacle. It arrives with steadiness. It stabilises the room, alters the atmosphere, and reminds the global community that leadership does not always manifest loudly, and that courage is not always conspicuous.

This is the courage of the female diplomat. This is what it means when truth enters the institution.

CHAPTER THREE

Gendered Protocols of Speech: Negotiating Voice and Authority in Patriarchal Diplomatic Environments

When Voice Becomes a Political Act

Diplomacy is often described as a universal language, a domain where every nation, delegate, and voice is accorded equal legitimacy. However, beneath this ideal lies a reality that female diplomats confront early in their careers: not all diplomatic environments are structured to accommodate a woman's voice. In some regions, cultural norms, patriarchal traditions, and deeply rooted social hierarchies dictate who is permitted to speak, who must remain silent, and whose presence is tolerated rather than embraced.

These standards do not cease to apply solely because she possesses a diplomatic passport. They accompany her into negotiation chambers, bilateral meetings, courtesy calls, and multilateral forums. Her mandate may be sovereign; however, her voice is moderated by centuries of expectation.

In some nations, a woman speaking in a room filled with men is regarded as inappropriate or culturally unacceptable. In others, she might be expected to communicate solely through a male colleague, even when she is the most senior official present. Within certain diplomatic cultures, her silence is not perceived as a strategic choice; rather, it is construed as compliance.

This is the landscape she must navigate well before articulating her inaugural words. Her voice becomes a political act, not merely a professional one.

A Room That Welcomes Her Presence but Hesitates at Her Voice

Manama welcomed her with warmth, an expression that acknowledged her presence with a gentle smile but exhibited hesitation when she spoke. First Secretary Amani Taha, a young Sudanese Nubian diplomat on her inaugural diplomatic assignment in an Arab nation, entered the bilateral meeting with a composed confidence cultivated through extensive preparation.

She was raised amidst two cultural worlds: the African rhythms inherent to her Nubian heritage and the Arab influences integral to Sudanese identity. She possessed a clear understanding of the region and upheld its traditions with respect. She conducted herself with the dignity befitting someone aware of both her historical responsibilities and the potential of her future. Yet nothing prepared her for the silence that awaited her.

The meeting began with polite greetings. Delegates exchanged titles and courteous acknowledgements. But when the substantive discussion began, every inquiry, comment, and request for clarification was directed to the junior male officer seated beside her. He shifted uncomfortably, glancing at her with the helplessness of someone caught between respect for hierarchy and the room's cultural expectations.

Amani remained composed. Senior female diplomats had warned her: "In some rooms, your voice will be too loud even when you haven't spoken." She understood the cultural protocol. She understood the gendered expectations.

She understood that her presence was accepted, but her voice was not.

Speaking Through Silence

Still, she had a mandate to deliver. When the host delegation asked about her country's position, the junior officer looked at her again, this time for guidance. She nodded slightly. He spoke, but the analysis, strategy, and nuance were entirely hers. Her expertise filled the room, even if her voice did not.

Later, as they walked out of the building, he whispered, "I'm sorry they didn't let you speak." She smiled, not out of resignation, but out of understanding.

"They heard me," she said softly. "They just didn't know it was me."

In that moment, she embodied the paradox of the female diplomat in patriarchal environments: to lead without appearing to lead, to speak through silence, to influence without violating cultural norms.

Her silence was not erasure.
It was a strategy.
It was diplomacy.
It was survival.

She understood that voice is not merely sound; it is power. And in some diplomatic cultures, power is gendered long before it is negotiated.

Mastering Dual Fluency

She therefore learned to master a complex set of skills. She discerned when silence was cultural respect and when it was erasure. She knew when to defer and when to insist. She recognised when her voice would destabilise the room and when it would steady it. She understood that speaking too soon could close doors, but speaking too late could weaken her mandate.

This was not weakness; it was institutional intelligence, the ability to navigate two systems simultaneously: the formal system of diplomacy and the informal system of gendered expectation.

In patriarchal diplomatic settings, she mastered the unspoken conventions: the sequence of address expected by men; the hierarchy that determines interruptions; the cultural significance of tone, posture, and eye contact; the prevailing expectation that she would be gentle, deferential, or unobtrusive, and the surprise when she was not.

She developed the ability to effectively interpret social dynamics with the strategic insight of a planner and the cultural sensitivity of an anthropologist. She acquired the skill to influence outcomes through precisely calibrated interventions, posing critical questions at strategic moments, providing clarifications at points of maximum impact, and delivering summaries that redefined dialogues without disrupting the existing cultural hierarchy.

Her voice became a diplomatic instrument, quiet, deliberate, and effective.

The Emotional Cost of Strategic Silence

Nevertheless, the emotional cost was tangible. There were instances when she experienced the weight of silence, not due to a lack of ability, but because her gender constrained her capacity to express it. Situations arose in which she was compelled to suppress her frustration to preserve the mission's dignity. There were moments when she needed to reconcile cultural respect with her personal truth. Additionally, there were times when she questioned whether the world would ever comprehend the silent struggles she endured within rooms where her voice was not intended to be heard.

But she continued.
Not because she was unbothered, but because she was committed.
Not because the system was fair, but because her presence was necessary.
Not because she was permitted to speak, but because she carried a nation that expected her to.

Her resilience was not loud. It was steady. It was disciplined. It was diplomatic.

Understanding the female diplomat requires recognising that her silence is never devoid of meaning. It embodies calculation, restraint, cultural sensitivity, and strategic patience. Her silence safeguards relationships, facilitates negotiations, and preserves the delicate equilibrium between respect and representation.

When she ultimately articulates her thoughts at the appropriate moment, in the suitable setting, after surpassing the cultural threshold, her words carry significant influence that demands attention. Her voice then transcends gender, embodying the voice of a nation.

Lessons Learned: Voice, Silence, and Authority

Amani's experience in Manama shows that silence can be a strategic tool rather than a sign of weakness. In particular contexts, silence sustains access and influence. Cultural respect does not require self-erasure.

Her analysis informed the negotiation, even when her contributions remained unacknowledged. Influence may be exerted indirectly. Voice is not always synonymous with volume; at times, the most impactful interventions modify the atmosphere without contravening established norms.

Her presence in the room itself constituted a form of politics; even in the absence of speech, she challenged traditional practices by simply being there.

Patriarchal environments necessitate dual fluency, requiring her to navigate both diplomatic and gendered expectations with accuracy.

Most importantly, her experience demonstrates that her voice is both disruptive and necessary. It challenges tradition even as it honours it. It expands what is possible without tearing at the fabric of cultural respect. It reminds the world that diplomacy is not only about power but also about presence, her presence, her authority, and her voice, even in the rooms where she is not meant to speak.

CHAPTER FOUR

Systems of Power: Internal Architectures of Foreign Service Bureaucracies

The Institution Behind the Illusion

Diplomacy is often imagined as a world of elegant receptions, strategic deliberations, and carefully negotiated accords. However, beneath this polished façade resides a complex institutional framework moulded by history, hierarchy, and deeply ingrained power dynamics. To comprehend the development of the female diplomat's career, it is essential first to understand the institution she joins: its structures, unwritten conventions, gatekeepers, and the implicit expectations that influence her path long before she utters her initial words in an international setting.

The diplomatic institution is not merely a workplace; it is a living organism.

It is defined by layers of tradition, ritual, and an almost sacred reverence for hierarchy. It possesses its own lexicon, rhythms, and ceremonial protocols. It rewards certain behaviour while quietly discouraging others. It is a system that remembers its past and safeguards its continuity.

Within this structured environment, the female diplomat must master not only her professional responsibilities but also the institutional codes that determine who is heard, trusted, and authorised to lead.

A System That Assesses Before It Accepts

Bern did not welcome her. Bern assessed her. For Minister Counsellor Lindiwe Okoroh, the institution revealed itself not through hostility but through scrutiny. Switzerland's capital, precise, orderly, and subtly hierarchical, mirrored the character of the foreign service itself.

During her first week, she attended a senior-level coordination meeting on this sensitive bilateral matter. This sensitive bilateral matter was approached with thorough preparation, supported by comprehensive data, contextual understanding, and a nuanced grasp of the political environment. Nonetheless, upon entering the room, a senior colleague signalled toward the rear and stated, "You may take notes for us today."

She paused, not out of confusion, but in strategic calculation.

Subsequently, she took her seat at the table, positioned her folder before her, and responded with composure, "I will contribute to the discussion. My analysis is central to this brief."

The atmosphere in the room shifted subtly yet perceptibly. Throughout the meeting, she articulated her points with clarity and precision, offering insights that redefined the discussion. By the end, the colleague who had initially tried to marginalise her leaned in and murmured, "Good intervention." Ms. Lindiwe did not smile; her purpose was not to seek validation but to assert her rightful place, which she had already earned, a common expectation for women in her professional environment.

Her intervention produced an immediate and notable impact.

The Ambassador requested that she serve as co-lead of the follow-up task team, and her analysis formed the foundation for the revised strategy. The institution gradually and hesitantly adapted to accommodate her presence.

Gatekeepers Seen and Unseen

For numerous women, the impact of the institution becomes apparent well before they entirely comprehend its structure. It commences with subtle indicators: the raised eyebrow upon her arrival, the presumption that she is an assistant rather than a delegate, and the courteous surprise expressed when she introduces herself as Counsellor, Ambassador, or Head of Chancery. These moments are not always malicious, but they are revealing. They expose the presence of gatekeepers, both individuals and systems, that regulate access, legitimacy, and belonging.

Gatekeepers in diplomacy are not always senior officials. Occasionally, they are colleagues responsible for managing information dissemination, administrators designated to control access to certain rooms, or cultural norms that determine who is permitted to speak first and whose expertise is acknowledged.

The female diplomat promptly understands that effective navigation within the institution necessitates more than mere competence. It requires institutional intelligence, the capacity to discern power dynamics, interpret unspoken rules, and distinguish between formal hierarchy and informal influence. The formal hierarchy is discernible through ranks, titles, reporting lines, and protocols.

Conversely, the informal hierarchy remains concealed, influenced by networks, alliances, loyalties, and the subtle authority exercised by those who have expertly navigated the system for many decades. She must comprehend both forms of hierarchy. She must be strategic in determining when to speak and when to remain silent, when to assert authority and when to permit the institution to elucidate its contradictions, and when to challenge or wait.

The institution conducts a thorough assessment of her capabilities before granting trust. It observes her responses to stress, her reactions to condescension, and her capacity to maintain a delicate balance between confidence and humility, an equilibrium expected to a greater extent than for her male counterparts. She is expected to be assertive without overstepping boundaries, knowledgeable without appearing threatening, confident without eliciting intimidation, and competent without causing disruption. Although these implicit expectations are not codified in any formal manual, they significantly influence her daily experiences.

Introducing Change Without Triggering Resistance

The institution values innovation but is cautious to avoid undermining authority. It accepts new ideas communicated through tradition, promotes leadership within comfort zones, and values subtle change. The female diplomat must implement change carefully, present new ideas without disruption, and lead without overstepping. Nonetheless, she provides a vital contribution to the institution: an alternative perspective. Her methodology for addressing conflict, grounded in empathy, active listening, and relational intelligence, adds humanity to diplomacy.

She introduces nuance into discussions that might otherwise be dominated by rigid posturing. She elucidates issues that require more than technical expertise. She reestablishes equilibrium in settings where the ego frequently eclipses purpose.

Nevertheless, her efforts are often undervalued. The institution resists recognising the intangible labour she performs, including the emotional labour of maintaining harmony, the intellectual labour involved in preparing for meetings where her ideas might be dismissed, and the relational labour of building trust across diverse cultures and personalities. Although these efforts are rarely reflected in performance evaluations, they are essential to diplomatic success.

She must also confront internal gatekeeping, the silent voice shaped by years of navigating environments that question her legitimacy. She must unlearn the belief that she must be twice as competent to gain recognition. She must resist the fear that any mistake will be exaggerated because of her gender. She must refuse to diminish herself in order to fit into spaces not designed for her. This internal gatekeeping is often the most challenging to dismantle.

Becoming a Quiet Architect of Institutional Change

Nonetheless, she persists. She establishes alliances with individuals who acknowledge her value. She identifies mentors who provide support without undermining her voice. She develops networks of women and men who comprehend that diplomacy is most effective when it embodies the diversity of the communities it serves. She acquires the skills to navigate the institution not as an outsider seeking validation, but as a leader influencing its future direction.

She discovers that systems can be navigated, hierarchies understood, and gatekeepers engaged with wisdom rather than fear. She realises that her presence is not an anomaly but an advancement. She understands that her voice, when rooted in truth and preparation, carries weight the institution cannot ignore. She also learns that even rigid institutions are not immune to transformation, especially when confronted with the quiet, persistent, unwavering strength of a woman confident in her purpose.

Lessons Learned: Navigating Systems of Power

Lindiwe's experience in Bern demonstrates that institutions tend to test before they trust, and that composed assertion can significantly influence perceptions within a formal setting. While gatekeeping remains a tangible barrier, it is possible to navigate it effectively. Informal power holds as much influence as formal hierarchy, and she has learned to interpret both. Competence alone is insufficient; it must be complemented by strategic assertion. Her analysis has redefined the bilateral strategy, and her presence has broadened the institution's understanding of leadership.

To understand the female diplomat, it is essential to recognise that her journey extends beyond mere representation of her nation. She must also navigate an institution still learning to accommodate her presence. She engages with systems not originally designed with her in mind, yet consistently finds ways to succeed within these frameworks. Her influence on the institution is as profound as the institution's influence on her, subtle, persistent, and irreversible.

Within the institution, she is not merely a participant; she is a presence, a force, and a quiet catalyst for transformation. With every room she enters, every system she navigates, and every gatekeeper she dispels through competence and clarity, she expands the boundaries of diplomacy.

CHAPTER FIVE

Career Pathways in Statecraft: The Structural Logic of Diplomatic Progression

The Architecture Beneath the Career

A diplomatic career is often described in terms of well-established functions: representing one's nation, advancing national interests, negotiating agreements, and safeguarding citizens abroad. However, beneath these general descriptions lies a complex framework that not only defines a diplomat's duties but also the identity she must cultivate to persist and succeed within the institution. For female diplomats, understanding this framework is vital; it forms the foundation upon which they must build their careers, professions, and resilient selves capable of bearing the burden of representation.

The framework begins long before her initial posting. It commences with examinations, interviews, and panel assessments designed to evaluate composure under pressure, analytical reasoning, communication skills, and adaptability. Nonetheless, there are also unspoken criteria, including perceptions of how well she aligns with the stereotypical image of a diplomat, assumptions regarding her reliability, and judgments concerning her ability to represent the state without attracting undue attention.

For many women, entering the foreign service is not merely an achievement; it is a crossing into a domain that was not originally designed with their presence in mind.

A Career Revealed Through Experience

Singapore welcomed her with meticulous precision, embodying a city where efficiency was not merely a value but an intrinsic rhythm. For Second Secretary Muna Kuku, the architecture of a diplomatic career became evident during her inaugural posting. She arrived eager, prepared, and resolutely committed to excellence. However, within a few weeks, she recognised that the institution’s structure was not merely formal but profoundly cultural, relational, and encoded.

Her Head of Mission entrusted her with coordinating a high-level economic delegation, a responsibility ordinarily reserved for more senior officers. An implicit question hung in the air: could she fulfil this duty? Muna approached the assignment with two fundamental tools: operational discipline and adaptive leadership. She mastered the city’s tempo, understood the host country’s expectations, and cultivated relationships with counterparts who initially underestimated her.

On the morning of the mission, a logistical crisis emerged. A pivotal meeting venue became inaccessible due to an unforeseen security lockdown. Senior officials panicked; however, Muna remained composed. Within sixty minutes, she recalibrated the schedule, secured an alternative venue, and renegotiated the engagement sequence. Upon the delegation's arrival, proceedings commenced smoothly. The crisis she had averted went unnoticed by others; the intricate organisation she maintained with quiet competence remained unseen. Nevertheless, her ambassador recognised her efforts, simply acknowledging, “Well done.”

In the subtle and understated realm of diplomacy, such recognition sufficed. Muna learned something essential that day: a diplomatic career is built not only on what is visible, but on the invisible scaffolding she holds in place.

The Formal and Informal Architecture

Upon entering the institution, the architecture reveals itself in successive layers. There is a formal structure comprising ranks, postings, departments, reporting lines, and performance reviews. It is well documented, methodical, and often characterised as meritocratic. Promotions follow a predetermined sequence. Organisational requirements, individual competencies, and timing govern assignments. On the surface, the arrangement seems orderly.

However, beneath the formal framework lies an informal network, the corridors where conversations influence reputations, the connections that affect recommendations, and the subtle labels assigned to officers: promising, difficult, solid, emotional, strong-willed. Although these labels are seldom documented, they circulate quickly. For female diplomats, a career can be shaped as profoundly by these whispers as by any formal assessment.

A diplomatic career typically follows a cyclical pattern: international assignments, reintegration at the headquarters, training, specialisation, and leadership roles. Each phase necessitates a distinct persona. During one assignment, an individual may assume the role of a political officer handling sensitive negotiations. In another context, she may serve as the head of chancery, overseeing staff, budgets, and crises. At headquarters, she might draft policies, coordinate multilateral positions, or provide counsel to senior officials. This rotation is deliberately structured to cultivate a versatile diplomatic officer.

Nevertheless, each rotation necessitates her reconstructing her life: relocating to a new country, adapting to a different culture, enrolling her children in a new school, integrating into an unfamiliar community, and meeting new expectations. The nature of these assignments is also temporal, measured in years rather than days. A posting is not merely a trip; it constitutes a season of life. Three years in one country, four in another, two at headquarters, followed by subsequent relocations. Over time, her life unfolds as a series of chapters characterised not only by personal milestones but also by professional assignments: the years spent in Geneva, the posting in Beijing, and the tenure at the mission in New York. Her career does not merely coexist with her life; it actively shapes its rhythm.

Gateways, Bottlenecks, and the Weight of Expectation

Within this organisational framework, there exist gateways and bottlenecks. Certain postings are regarded as career-defining, strategic capitals, multilateral hubs, and crisis zones. These roles facilitate accelerated promotion, enhance visibility, and broaden influence. Conversely, others, although demanding, are considered peripheral. It is incumbent upon the female diplomat to develop the ability to discern which assignments serve her professional advancement and which subtly hinder her progress. She must determine when to accept a posting for strategic purposes and when to select one based on considerations of survival, familial commitments, or mental well-being.

There are unspoken expectations embedded within this framework: the obligation to be available at all hours, to relocate when the institution does, even if her family is unprepared, to adapt to any environment regardless of its isolating nature, and to absorb the emotional impact of crises without overt strain. Although these expectations are not exclusive to women, they affect their bodies, relationships, and sense of identity in distinctive ways.

Over time, she develops an internal architecture, a framework for integrating the many roles she must play. She becomes a mediator between multiple worlds: her home culture and the host country, political mandates and human realities, institutional demands and personal principles. She learns to compartmentalise when necessary, to protect what is sacred, and to let go of what she cannot control.

She also learns that diplomacy rests on both visibility and invisibility. There are moments when she stands at the centre of the room, delivering statements, leading delegations, and hosting events. And there are long stretches of unseen work, drafting briefs late into the night, preparing talking points for others to deliver, and managing crises that never reach the news. The institution depends on this invisible labour. For the female diplomat, much of her contribution lies here.

Leadership and the Shifting Architecture

As her career progresses, the architectural framework continues to evolve. Leadership introduces new responsibilities: overseeing teams, mentoring junior officers, and representing not only her country but also the institution. She becomes, whether intentionally or not, a symbol of what women can accomplish in diplomacy. Younger officers see in her a pathway that previously did not exist.

Nevertheless, even at senior levels, the architectural structure remains incomplete. There are spaces where she is the sole woman. Decision-making continues in environments from which she is excluded. Assumptions about her leadership style, tone, and presence persist. The architectural evolution proceeds slowly. She lives in the tension between the current state and potential futures.

Comprehending the architecture of a diplomatic career requires recognising that it functions both as a structure and as a narrative. The structure shapes her career trajectory; the narrative gives her perseverance significance. It is a system that demands commitment, and a vocation that gives these demands purpose. She learns to exercise agency not by dismantling the architecture instantly but by inhabiting it differently, with clarity, integrity, and quiet persistence. With each posting, negotiation, and discreet act of competence, she reshapes the institution's perception of what a diplomat can embody.

The architecture may not have been built with her in mind, but it cannot remain unchanged once she has walked through it.

Lessons Learned: The Logic of Progression

Muna's experience in Singapore shows that a diplomatic career is shaped as much by invisible labour as by visible achievement. The institution tests before it trusts, and competence must be paired with composure, adaptability, and strategic clarity. The architecture of progression is both formal and informal, and she must learn to navigate both with intelligence and intention.

Her journey shows that a diplomatic career is not merely a sequence of roles but a life lived at the intersection of duty and identity, structure and vocation, institution and self. The architecture may impose constraints, but it also provides a foundation on which she builds something unprecedented, a mode of service that is profoundly competent, deeply human, and quietly transformative.

CHAPTER SIX

Operational Mandates Beyond the Job Description: Unwritten Expectations in Diplomacy

The Unwritten Job Description

Every profession has an official job description, a well-organised list of duties, responsibilities, and expectations. Diplomacy is no exception. Recruitment brochures set out the core pillars: representing the state, negotiating agreements, safeguarding citizens, promoting national interests, and managing bilateral and multilateral relationships. While precise, these descriptions remain incomplete; they illustrate the role's architecture but fail to capture its internal intricacies. They outline the visible structure but neglect the hidden scaffolding that sustains the profession.

The actual job description, the one diplomat's experience rather than merely reading, remains unwritten. It is acquired through crises, shaped by experience, and discreetly transmitted within the institution. For female diplomats, this implicit dimension is often even more subtle, demanding, and emotionally complex than the institution readily acknowledges.

A Crisis That Reveals the Real Work

Nairobi extended a warm welcome, the kind of warmth that softens the edges of difficult days. For Consular Officer Lee Shim, the unwritten job description revealed itself not in a conference room but in a moment of crisis.

A bus accident involving multiple citizens occurred on the outskirts of the city. Telephones rang incessantly.

Families were frantic.

Headquarters demanded hourly updates.

Local authorities were overwhelmed.

Shim approached the situation utilising two essential instruments: emotional stability and crisis management. She coordinated with hospitals, reassured families, and negotiated access to information that would otherwise have remained inaccessible. She managed the emotions present in the environment and those directed towards her. She maintained composure amidst panic without internalising it. She established a space where grief could be expressed without compromising the integrity of the operation.

By nightfall, every citizen had been accounted for. No press release mentioned her name. No report conveyed the emotional burden she bore. However, this unseen labour constituted the true responsibilities. Shim understood what every female diplomat eventually discovers: the role they perform but are not officially informed about is the one that ultimately defines them.

The Emotional Labour

The unwritten responsibilities begin with emotional labour. Diplomacy demands the ability to absorb tension silently, to maintain composure when others lose theirs, to preserve dignity when confronted with disrespect. It requires listening beyond words, interpreting unspoken fears, and responding with restraint even when provoked.

Emotional steadiness is not explicitly listed as a competency; however, it is fundamental to diplomatic success. Female diplomats experience a significantly heightened requirement for emotional labour. They must manage not only the emotions evident within the official setting but also those projected onto them. Their composure may be misinterpreted as fragility, their assertiveness as hostility, and their silence as ignorance.

They are compelled to continually adjust their tone, posture, and facial expressions, not due to a lack of confidence, but because they are aware that their presence is perceived through a gendered lens. This continuous self-monitoring becomes an inherent aspect of their role, despite its lack of formal acknowledgement.

Adaptability as a Daily Mandate

Adaptability is another implicit prerequisite. Diplomacy requires the ability to move swiftly between diverse functions, including drafting policy documents, negotiating treaties, conducting technical analysis, demonstrating human empathy, responding to crises, and carrying out ceremonial duties. She must understand political dynamics, cultural subtleties, and institutional priorities, all while maintaining her personal identity.

However, adaptability extends beyond mere professionalism; it is fundamentally personal. The diplomat must repeatedly reconstruct her life, adapting to new countries, households, communities, and routines. She must learn to thrive in unfamiliar environments, often without the support systems she previously relied upon. For the female diplomat, this frequently involves navigating loneliness, balancing familial responsibilities across continents, and managing the emotional burden of continual transition.

These realities are not enumerated within any official job description, yet they shape her daily existence.

Invisible Leadership That Shapes Outcomes

The unarticulated dimension of her role also involves an unseen form of leadership. Diplomats influence outcomes well before formal negotiations commence. They discreetly mediate conflicts, foster relationships that prevent crises, and assume responsibility for representing their nations in every interaction, from high-level official meetings to informal conversations at receptions.

For the female diplomat, invisible leadership constitutes both a strength and a burden. She often leads through empathy, clarity, and relational intelligence, qualities essential to diplomacy yet rarely acknowledged. She detects tensions before they escalate, redefines conversations to establish common ground, and offers insights that influence the course of negotiations.

Nevertheless, her contributions may be attributed to others or dismissed as "soft skills." She must learn to lead without waiting for recognition, to influence without seeking acknowledgement, and to trust that her impact remains significant even when it is not immediately apparent.

Resilience as a Silent Requirement

Resilience is another implicit requirement. Diplomacy exposes her to crises, conflicts, and human suffering. She may respond to emergencies involving citizens abroad, support colleagues in distress, or manage the emotional aftermath of political instability.

She must maintain composure even when the stakes are high or the consequences are personal. She must bear the emotional burden of her responsibilities without letting it overwhelm her. Resilience also means enduring the institution's internal challenges, the slow pace of change, subtle biases, and implicit hierarchies. It means continuing to show up even when her contributions are overlooked, her expertise questioned, or her presence minimised. It means holding fast to her purpose even when the institution does not fully recognise her.

Representation Beyond the Conference Room

The unwritten job description extends beyond explicit duties. A diplomat embodies her nation not solely during official meetings but also through every interaction, social event, community gathering, and informal conversation. She becomes a symbol of her country's values, culture, and identity.

For the female diplomat, this role carries additional significance. She symbolises potential for women domestically, challenges stereotypes internationally, and serves as a reminder that leadership may take forms different from conventional expectations. She must navigate cultural expectations that may conflict with her personal identity. Additionally, she must balance authenticity with diplomacy, assertiveness with tact, and confidence with humility. Her representation of her country requires grace, even when she is exhausted, emotionally drained, or quietly struggling.

This ongoing performance of national identity is part of the job, though it is rarely acknowledged.

Unspoken Sacrifices

Unspoken duties also encompass sacrifice. Diplomacy necessitates time, presence, and emotional dedication. It compels her to forgo family milestones, to oversee long-distance relationships, to raise children in unfamiliar settings, or to choose between career progression and personal stability. These sacrifices are not exclusive to women; however, societal expectations often impose a greater burden upon them.

She must learn to bear guilt without allowing it to overwhelm her, to maintain love across distances, and to construct a life that is both meaningful and adaptable. She must forgive herself for those moments when she cannot be present everywhere at once. This emotional balancing act is intrinsic to her role, yet no one provides her with explicit preparation for it.

Purpose as the Anchor of the Unwritten Role

Ultimately, the unwritten job description is rooted in purpose. Diplomacy transcends merely being a profession; it is a vocation. It requires a commitment to causes greater than oneself, including peace, justice, national service, and global cooperation.

This purpose sustains her during periods when the institution is slow to adapt, when sacrifices accumulate, and when recognition remains scarce.

The female diplomat approaches her duties with quiet resilience. She recognises that her presence holds significance even when it is not acknowledged. She understands that her voice wields influence even when it is not heard. She acknowledges that her work influences the world in ways that may never be publicly recognised.

Furthermore, she is aware that the unwritten responsibilities, emotional labour, adaptability, invisible leadership, resilience, representation, and sacrifice are not burdens but rather manifestations of her capacity.

They reveal her strength.
They reveal her wisdom.
They reveal her subtle authority.
And they make her presence not only necessary, but transformative.

Lessons Learned

The experience in Nairobi reveals that the unwritten responsibilities of diplomacy are often what define the effectiveness of female diplomats. Emotional stability, adaptability, covert leadership, and resilience constitute the true foundation of her efforts, despite their omission from formal job descriptions. She recognises that diplomacy is upheld not only by policy and protocol but also by the emotional labour she discreetly and consistently performs. Her capacity to absorb tension without succumbing to it, to adapt without losing her sense of self, and to lead without seeking acknowledgement exemplifies mastery.

These unspoken expectations shape her identity as a diplomat, instructing her that the most impactful aspects of her service are often the least visible. Through this concealed labour, she realises that diplomacy transcends mere profession to become a vocation grounded in humanity, empathy, and the quiet strength necessary to bear the emotional burdens of representation.

CHAPTER SEVEN

Pioneering in Foreign Service

The Weight of Being the First

There is a significant burden on those who are first, sole, or among a select few. In the sphere of diplomacy, this burden transcends mere symbolism; it is actively experienced. It shapes perceptions of female diplomats, influences how their voices are received, and moulds expectations of their performance well before they have the opportunity to demonstrate their capabilities. The institution venerates its appointments as milestones; however, beneath the outward celebration lies a quieter reality: the path they navigate is unpaved, expectations are heightened, and the scrutiny they face is incessant.

Ottawa received her with a demeanour that demanded discipline. Ambassador Camila Rojas of Chile recently assumed a position that had not previously been held by a woman from her country. The congratulations extended were sincere, yet beneath them persisted an underlying tone: you are the first. The institution regarded this as progress; nonetheless, Camila perceived the deeper truth, that she was entering a space not originally designed with her inclusion in mind.

Her initial week made this evident. During a high-level briefing, a senior official glanced at her nameplate and then at her face, remarking, "We were expecting the ambassador." Camila responded with a gentle smile, stating, "You are." The atmosphere shifted, not with hostility but with surprise. She perceived the weight settle upon her shoulders: the weight of being the first. She delivered her briefing with clarity and precision, anticipating questions before they arose, grounding her arguments in data and foresight.

By the end, the same official who had doubted her approached with a quiet, reluctant respect. As she stepped back into the cold air outside, she realised an essential truth: when you are the first, you do not merely perform the role; you redefine it.

The Responsibility That Arrives Uninvited

Being the first is not merely a milestone; it constitutes an unwelcome responsibility. She becomes a representative not only of her nation but also of all women who will follow. Her achievements are magnified, yet her mistakes are equally scrutinised. Her presence is celebrated, yet subject to critical examination. She is expected to excel not solely for herself but also to uphold the institution's narrative of progress.

This implicit expectation accompanies her at all times. It begins early, in the subtle admiration conveyed through congratulatory messages, in the institution's pride in its evolution, and in the underlying truth: she is entering a space that has yet to learn how to receive her. She must understand the rules while simultaneously challenging them. She must fulfil the role while reshaping it. She must embody the aspirations of many while managing the doubts of a few.

The Solitude of Being the Only One

Being the only woman in the room carries its own gravity. It is a solitude that is both visible and invisible. In meetings, she notices the absence of others who share her lived experience. In decision-making forums, she senses assumptions shaped by perspectives different from her own. She becomes acutely aware of her presence, her tone, her posture, knowing she is not merely representing herself but embodying a broader possibility.

She develops a heightened sensitivity to the atmosphere. She recognises when her ideas are dismissed prematurely. She notices when her expertise is scrutinised more intensely than her colleagues'. She senses when her presence disrupts unspoken norms. She learns to anticipate resistance, not because she doubts her capabilities, but because experience has taught her that legitimacy must be earned repeatedly. Proof of competence becomes a continuous requirement.

Among the Few, Yet Still an Exception

Being among the few carries its own complexities. There is comfort in seeing another woman across the table, yet an awareness that their presence remains an exception. They exchange glances that communicate mutual understanding, a shared experience of navigating a system still adjusting to their inclusion. They support each other discreetly, recognising that solidarity is not optional but essential. Yet even in these moments of connection, they remain aware that the institution continues to regard them as anomalies.

The burden of being the first, the only, or among the few extends inward. It shapes her self-perception, making her more cautious, more deliberate, and more conscious of the repercussions of each action. She carries the fear of reinforcing stereotypes, the pressure to exceed expectations, and the anxiety of being judged not as an individual but as a representative of her gender.

She learns to steady her voice even when doubt murmurs beneath it. She learns to stand her ground even when uncertainty flickers within. This internal burden is substantial, yet it becomes a catalyst for transformation. It sharpens her discernment, strengthens her resilience, and deepens her sense of purpose. She learns to navigate complexity with composure, respond to bias with clarity, and lead with a quiet authority that does not depend on external validation. Her development into a diplomat is shaped not only by training but also by endurance.

Change and Diversity

Yet this burden is not hers alone. It is shaped by the institution, its history, its culture, and its pace of change. The institution celebrates diversity, yet often hesitates to dismantle the structures that hinder it. It welcomes women into its ranks, yet does not consistently remove the barriers that impede their advancement. It values representation, yet rarely acknowledges the emotional labour required to sustain it. The female diplomat must navigate this paradox daily.

Still, she persists.

She persists because she understands the significance of her presence. Her perseverance is driven by the knowledge that her visibility creates opportunities for others.

She remains committed to diplomacy and service, believing in the possibility of a more inclusive institution. Her steadfastness is rooted in a calling that transcends the obstacles she encounters.

Becoming a Pioneer

Her persistence elevates her from being the first, the only, or among the few to something more enduring: a pioneer. She becomes a quiet architect of institutional change, a symbol of what can be achieved when courage aligns with opportunity. Her presence shifts perceptions. Her leadership challenges assumptions. Her voice broadens the scope of inclusion within diplomacy.

Although the burden she bears is considerable, it does not define her alone. She takes pride in standing where others could not, in becoming the exemplar she once sought, and in demonstrating that the institution is capable of evolution.

Her purpose is to shape a system that will one day welcome women without hesitation. Her legacy is to pave the way for those who will follow. Being the first, the only, or among the few is not a role she chooses; it is one she inherits. Yet she bears it with dignity, strength, and a quiet courage that transforms the institution from within. And because of her, another woman will one day step into the room and experience something she never had: the reassurance of not standing alone.

Lessons Learned

Camila's experience in Ottawa reveals that being the first, the only, or among the few is not merely a professional milestone but an emotional and institutional burden. She learns that pioneering in diplomacy requires a dual consciousness: the awareness of her own competence and of how her presence unsettles longstanding assumptions. Her journey teaches her that legitimacy is not granted automatically; it is earned repeatedly, often in rooms where her authority is questioned before she speaks. She discovers that the solitude of being the only woman in the room sharpens her discernment, strengthens her resilience, and deepens her understanding of leadership. She also learns that institutional progress is not synonymous with institutional readiness.

The applause that accompanies her appointment does not erase the biases she must navigate. Yet she recognises that her presence itself is a form of transformation, a quiet, steady disruption of inherited norms. Her perseverance becomes a pathway for others, her composure a counter-narrative to doubt, and her leadership a testament to what is possible when courage meets opportunity.

Ultimately, she learns that pioneering is not about being celebrated; it is about creating space where none existed. It is about carrying the weight of representation with dignity, reshaping the institution through presence, and ensuring that the next woman who enters the room does so with less hesitation and more belonging.

Through her journey, she understands that being the first is not a burden she carries alone; it is a legacy she builds for those who will follow.

CHAPTER EIGHT

Presence as Policy: The Politics of Visibility in International Engagement

Presence as a Political Act

Presence is often described as a simple fact, the act of being physically present in a room, attending meetings, or appearing where duty necessitates. However, within the realm of diplomacy, presence is never devoid of meaning. It conveys intent, significance, and repercussions. It constitutes a political action. For a female diplomat, presence extends beyond mere physicality; it becomes a form of negotiation, communication, and, at times, a silent challenge to prevailing assumptions. Her presence is not simply observed; it is interpreted, assessed, and often contested.

Vienna welcomed her with understated elegance, its refined formality masking underlying hierarchies beneath polished surfaces.

For Minister Plenipotentiary Sofia Almeida of Portugal, the political ramifications of her presence became clear on her first day at the multilateral mission. She participated in a high-level coordination meeting where each seat appeared to bear historical significance, hierarchical importance, and claims to authority. As she assumed her position at the table, a senior delegate examined her badge and inquired, “Are you here to support your ambassador?” Sofia maintained steady eye contact. “I am here to represent my country,” she responded, placing her folder on the table with deliberate purpose.

The atmosphere shifted subtly but unmistakably. Her presence had already commenced its negotiation. Throughout the meeting, she spoke sparingly but with precision, offering insights that reframed the discussion. When she concluded, the same delegate who had questioned her legitimacy leaned back, observing her with a reluctant respect.

Sofia recognised the moment for what it was: in diplomacy, presence is the first negotiation, and often the most political.

The First Negotiation

The politics of presence begin the moment she enters the institution. Her arrival is not merely an additional appointment; it signifies a shift within the landscape. She embodies a demographic traditionally absent or underrepresented. Her presence confronts assumptions regarding who belongs in diplomacy, who represents the nation, and who wields authority. Even before she speaks, her presence disrupts the established choreography of power.

In numerous contexts, her presence becomes the initial stage of negotiation. She advocates for her right to be acknowledged as competent, to be heard without interruption, to speak without interrogation, and to occupy space without apology. These negotiations are subtle and often unnoticed by those unfamiliar with such experiences. Nonetheless, she perceives them physically, through her posture, the meticulous arrangement of her documents, and the anticipation of questions intended to test her legitimacy. Her presence assumes a political dimension because it is constantly subject to evaluation.

Symbolism, Substance, and the Struggle for Influence

The politics of presence influence her positioning within the institution. She may be invited to meetings as a symbolic gesture, a sign of advancement. However, symbolism does not confer influence. She must discern whether her inclusion is based on expertise or optics. She must balance accepting visibility with insisting on substantive participation. She must learn to translate symbolic presence into genuine influence, an influence that shapes decisions rather than merely maintaining decorum.

Protocol becomes another arena in which presence carries political significance. Seating arrangements, speaking order, and access to information reflect underlying power structures. She quickly understands that her seat is not merely logistical but also communicative. A seat at the periphery sends one message; a seat at the centre sends another. She must interpret these signals with acuity, recognising that protocol is not merely ceremonial but strategic choreography.

Her presence is political because it is often unexpected. In some cultural contexts, her authority is questioned solely based on her gender. In others, her appearance challenges deeply ingrained beliefs about leadership. She must navigate these domains with sensitivity and resilience, asserting her legitimacy while respecting local norms. She must project confidence without inciting defensiveness and maintain humility without diminishing her authority.

This balance constitutes part of the politics of presence, a skill developed through experience, intuition, and emotional intelligence.

Presence in the Eyes of Colleagues and the Institution

The politics of presence extend to her interactions with colleagues. A female Diplomat may encounter allies who support her, mentors who guide her, and peers who respect her. However, she may also face subtle or overt resistance. Some may question her qualifications; others may underestimate her; and a few may feel threatened by her competence. She must navigate these dynamics with grace, discerning when to confront, when to ignore, and when to exercise strategic restraint. Her presence becomes a quiet assertion of her right to occupy spaces not originally designed for her.

Nevertheless, presence is more than mere visibility. It embodies the impression she leaves behind. A female Diplomat recognizes that her presence must endure, not through force, but through clarity, consistency, and integrity. She must articulate with precision, act with purpose, and comport herself with dignity. Her contributions should remain influential long after her departure. This encapsulates the essence of the politics of presence: the capacity to influence without spectacle, to shift outcomes without demanding undue attention.

The Emotional Weight of Being Seen

Presence carries emotional weight. A female Diplomat represents not only her country but also women like her, women who aspire to her position, women who were told diplomacy was not for them, women who have never seen themselves reflected in these spaces. Her presence becomes a form of advocacy, even when she does not intend it. She embodies possibility. She demonstrates that leadership can be quiet, steady, and profoundly human.

But the politics of presence is not only external; it is also internal. She must confront her own doubts, fears, and insecurities. She must silence the voice that questions whether she belongs, whether she is enough, or whether she is prepared. She must cultivate an internal presence, a sense of belonging that does not depend on external validation. This internal presence becomes her anchor in environments where she may feel outnumbered, underestimated, or unseen.

Voice as an Extension of Presence

The politics of presence also shape how she uses her voice. She recognises that timing is as crucial as content. She understands that silence can serve strategic purposes, that attentive listening wields power, and that a single carefully chosen sentence can change the trajectory of a meeting. She acknowledges that presence is not measured by the frequency of speech but by the intentionality behind her words. Her voice becomes an instrument, measured, deliberate, and grounded in truth.

Presence is inherently relational.

She builds alliances not through coercion but through trust.

She nurtures relationships across cultures, institutions, and individuals. She understands that diplomacy extends beyond policy; it fundamentally concerns people.

Her presence acts as a bridge, easing tensions, aligning perspectives, and encouraging dialogue. This relational presence exerts political influence by shaping outcomes in ways that formal authority alone cannot.

Presence in Moments of Crisis

The politics of presence are most evident in moments of crisis. When tensions escalate, negotiations stall, or emotions run high, A female Diplomat's presence becomes a stabilising force. She brings calm to chaos, clarity to confusion, and dignity to conflict. Her presence offers reassurance, grounding, and guidance. In such moments, presence transcends politics; it becomes transformational.

Yet the politics of presence carry costs. She must continually manage perceptions, expectations, and assumptions. She shoulders the emotional burden of being both visible and invisible. She must balance authenticity with diplomacy, vulnerability with resilience. She must protect her inner world while engaging fully with external demands.

This emotional labour is part of the politics of presence, though it is rarely acknowledged.

Presence as Transformation

Nevertheless, she continues to persevere. Her perseverance is driven by the understanding that presence constitutes power, not through loudness or aggression, but through consistency and unmistakable resolve. Her perseverance is founded on the conviction that her presence broadens the scope of what is attainable. She remains dedicated because she believes in the work, the calling, and the purpose that have led her to diplomacy. Her persistence is firmly grounded in an unshakable truth that cannot be suppressed.

Ultimately, the politics of presence is not merely a burden she bears; it is a vital force in the evolution of diplomacy. Her presence reshapes the institution, challenges assumptions, expands perspectives, creates new opportunities, and alters the environment simply by being there. The politics of presence reveal a profound truth: leadership is not only authority but authenticity; influence is not only volume but clarity; power is not only dominance but presence itself.

In every room she enters, the female diplomat demonstrates that presence, quiet, steady, and intentional, is one of the most powerful acts of political agency.

Lesson Learnt

Sofia's experience in Vienna illustrates that presence is not a passive state but an active form of diplomacy. She recognises that simply entering a room can alter its dynamics, challenge existing assumptions, and redefine its expectations. Her presence becomes her initial form of negotiation, a negotiation for legitimacy, recognition, and the right to be heard without precondition. She concludes that visibility bears political significance, that protocol conveys authority, and that silence can be as strategic as speech.

Furthermore, she learns that presence is relational. It is influenced by the alliances she constructs, the trust she fosters, and the stability she introduces into tense or uncertain situations. Her presence serves as a bridge connecting different cultures, personalities, and institutional histories. Through this experience, she comprehends that diplomacy extends beyond policy to encompass the human capacity to influence through authenticity, clarity, and composure.

Most importantly, she learns that presence is internal before it is external. She must cultivate an inner steadiness that does not depend on validation, an inner confidence that does not waver under scrutiny, and an inner clarity that guides her voice. This internal presence becomes her anchor in rooms where she may be underestimated or unseen.

Ultimately, Sofia's journey teaches her that presence, quiet, intentional, and unwavering, is one of the most powerful diplomatic tools she possesses. It enables her to shape outcomes without force, command respect without raising her voice, and expand what is possible simply by standing firmly in who she is.

CHAPTER NINE

The Diplomacy of Micro-Decisions: Quiet Leadership in Foreign Service Practice

Leadership in the Smallest Movements

The true essence of diplomacy is not confined to grand negotiations or high-level summits. It is revealed in the discreet, routine decisions diplomats make daily, so subtle they rarely attract attention yet so impactful they shape the tone, trajectory, and integrity of entire missions. These decisions are nuanced, deliberate, and deeply human. They demand sound judgement, emotional sensitivity, and a constant awareness of the responsibilities inherent in representation. They constitute the quiet architecture of leadership.

Seoul instilled discipline in her, while Wellington instilled softness.

For Counsellor Ji-Woo Han of South Korea, the diplomacy of everyday decisions did not manifest in dramatic moments but in the subtle choices she made each morning at the mission in New Zealand. During her first week, a minor misunderstanding arose between two departments: an email was misinterpreted, a delayed response was taken personally, and the tone sounded sharper than intended. Such issues, if left unaddressed, can quietly undermine trust.

Ji-Woo paused before replying. She reread the messages. She considered each officer's personality, cultural background, and the pressures they were under. Then she made a simple yet strategic decision: instead of replying by email, she walked to each office in person. Her presence softened defensiveness.

Her tone diffused tension. Her clarity restored alignment. By the end of the day, the issue had resolved itself, not through authority, but through a micro-decision grounded in emotional intelligence. Ji-Woo recognised an essential truth: *diplomacy extends far beyond conference rooms. It is exercised in the quiet decisions that prevent minor fissures from becoming fractures.*

The Daily Decisions That Define Her

For Ji-Woo, daily choices transcend administrative tasks; they become acts of representation. They embody national identity, reflect personal values, demonstrate discernment, and reveal her understanding of the delicate balance between firmness and grace. She knows that even the smallest decision can influence her nation's reputation, strengthen or weaken relationships, and build or erode trust.

The diplomacy of daily decision-making begins the moment she enters her office. She must determine which issues require immediate attention and which can wait. She must interpret a colleague's tone, read signals from the host country, and manage misunderstandings before they escalate. She must decide when to speak, when to listen, when to intervene, and when to observe. Individually, these choices may seem trivial; collectively, they reveal her leadership.

One of her most consequential daily decisions concerns the use of her voice. In meetings, she must decide whether to assert her perspective early or wait until the room stabilises. She must judge whether speaking now will advance the discussion or provoke resistance. She must recognise when silence is strategic and when silence becomes acquiescence. Her voice is not merely a means of communication; it is a symbol of clarity and confidence.

Each time she speaks, she shapes not only the conversation but also how her authority is perceived. Another daily decision concerns relationships. Diplomacy rests on human interaction with colleagues, host country officials, international partners, and local communities. She must decide how to cultivate these relationships with sincerity and professionalism. She must know when to show warmth and when to maintain distance. She must build trust without compromising boundaries. These relational decisions require emotional intelligence, cultural sensitivity, and a deep understanding of human behaviour.

Conflict, Interpretation, and the Quiet Work of Stability

The diplomacy of micro-decisions significantly influences her approach to conflict management. Not all disputes are dramatic; many are subtle, such as a misinterpreted email, a delayed response, or a tone perceived as dismissive. She must decide whether to address the issue directly or let it pass without intervention. Furthermore, she must evaluate whether the tension originates from misunderstandings, cultural differences, or deeper institutional dynamics. She is tasked with choosing whether to escalate the matter, mediate, or absorb the conflict. Such decisions require maturity, patience, and the ability to look beyond the surface.

Leadership is also demonstrated through quotidian decisions. She must decide how to motivate her team, provide constructive feedback without discouraging, acknowledge effort, and foster an environment where individuals feel valued. Additionally, she must decide when to delegate tasks and when to assume responsibility personally. It is essential to balance compassion with accountability.

These decisions collectively exert a more profound influence on the culture of her mission than any formal directive. An additional aspect of everyday diplomacy pertains to her interpretation of information. Diplomats are consistently exposed to data, reports, briefings, conversations, and observations. She must determine what is pertinent, what constitutes noise, what necessitates verification, and what calls for action. It is essential to differentiate between fact and perception, urgency and distraction. Her capacity to interpret information accurately constitutes one of her most significant daily decisions, thereby shaping policy, strategy, and national interests.

Even her demeanour is a deliberate diplomatic choice. Her demeanour is not superficial; it constitutes an integral part of her professional repertoire. She must decide how to present herself in formal, informal, tense, or celebratory contexts. She must convey confidence without arrogance, warmth without vulnerability, and neutrality without detachment. Her presence communicates as much as her words. Every gesture, expression, and pause is intentional.

Gendered Expectations and Ethical Anchors

For the female diplomat, quotidian decisions are influenced by gendered expectations. She must navigate assumptions regarding her competence, authority, and emotional capacity. She must determine how to respond to subtle biases, whether to confront, overlook, or redirect them. She must maintain her authenticity while adapting to environments that may not entirely acknowledge her. These choices necessitate courage, wisdom, and a robust sense of self.

Ethical decisions are also part of her daily diplomacy. She must uphold integrity in environments where shortcuts are tempting. She must represent her country honestly while navigating political sensitivities. She must balance transparency with discretion. These decisions shape her character and define her legacy.

The Quiet Architecture of Leadership

The diplomacy of micro-decisions may lack glamour or recognition, but it is the foundation of effective foreign service. It sustains relationships, prevents crises, and builds trust. It requires consistency, humility, and emotional steadiness. It is shaped by her values, experiences, mentors, and the lessons she has quietly absorbed over time. She knows that diplomacy is not only in grand gestures. It is in how she responds to unexpected questions, manages difficult colleagues, reads subtle tones, and chooses kindness without compromising strength. It is in how she balances clarity with empathy, and firmness with grace.

Her leadership is most evident in these daily decisions, not to the world at large, but to those who work alongside her, rely on her, and learn from her. These decisions illuminate her character, discipline, and discernment. They demonstrate that diplomacy is not merely a profession; it is a way of being.

Ultimately, the diplomacy of micro-decisions forms the foundation of her effectiveness, credibility, and quiet authority. It allows her to navigate complexity with composure, build trust through authentic interaction, and represent her nation with dignity. It elevates her from simply executing diplomacy to embodying it, one deliberate choice at a time.

Lesson Learnt

Ji Woo's experience in Wellington demonstrates that diplomacy is maintained not through grand gestures but through subtle, deliberate choices that define the rhythm of a mission. She recognises that leadership is reflected in minor decisions, in how she manages tension, interprets tone, chooses presence over distance, and employs her voice with purpose rather than spontaneity. These micro-decisions serve as true indicators of her maturity as a diplomat, illustrating that influence often manifests in subtle moments beyond public recognition.

Furthermore, she understands that emotional intelligence is integral to diplomatic work, not merely an accessory. Her capacity to read a room, anticipate conflicts, and restore harmony without escalation constitutes quiet authority. Through her daily choices, she learns that diplomacy extends beyond representing her nation; it involves fostering an environment conducive to trust, where misunderstandings are resolved, and relationships are strengthened.

Most critically, she realises that the discipline of micro-decisions shapes her character as significantly as her career pursuits. Each decision, when to speak, listen, intervene, or withdraw, refines her judgment and deepens her understanding of leadership. She concludes that diplomacy is not confined to formal settings but is embodied in everyday interactions that shape a mission's culture.

This insight reveals that quiet leadership is not subordinate but foundational to effective diplomacy.

CHAPTER TEN

Emotional Labour in State Representation: The Hidden Demands of the Role

The Weight of Representation

Buenos Aires had prepared her for elegance, but Pretoria introduced her to the emotional gravity of state representation. For Deputy Consul Mariana Duarte, the emotional burden of diplomacy did not emerge in grand crises but in the quiet, human moments that rarely appear in official reports. Her first month brought a case involving a young Argentine student hospitalised after a severe accident. The family called every hour, their voices trembling with fear. Headquarters demanded updates. Local authorities moved slowly under pressure.

Mariana became the bridge between fear and bureaucracy, between a mother's trembling voice and the rigid pace of institutional procedure. She reassured the family with a steadiness she did not always feel. She negotiated with overwhelmed hospital administrators, pressed for clarity, and translated medical uncertainty into language the family could bear. When the mother whispered, "Please… just tell me my daughter is alive," Mariana felt the weight settle in her chest.

When the call ended, she closed her office door and let silence wash over her. This was the moment she understood what every female diplomat eventually learns: representation is not only political; it is profoundly emotional.

The Emotional Architecture of Diplomatic Work

Beneath the formal definitions of diplomacy lies an unspoken truth: A diplomat naturally becomes the emotional anchor of her mission as she carries the fears, frustrations, and expectations of citizens, colleagues, and institutions.

Mariana learned quickly that emotional regulation was not optional; it was operational. She had to remain composed despite exhaustion, patient despite irritation, and gracious despite disrespect. She absorbed others' emotions without allowing them to destabilise her. She became a vessel for anxieties she did not create and a conduit for emotions that were not her own.

Her emotional landscape became a terrain to be navigated carefully. She had to decide which emotions to reveal and which to conceal. Vulnerability could be strategic, but it could also be dangerous. Empathy was essential, but boundaries were a matter of survival.

This emotional discipline was nowhere in her job description, yet it shaped every interaction she had.

Gendered Expectations and Invisible Labour

For the female diplomat, emotional labour is intensified by gendered expectations. Mariana noticed it immediately. She was the one colleagues approached to mediate tensions. She was the one distressed citizen whom the others gravitated toward, and she was expected to "soften" difficult conversations, soothe frustrations, and maintain harmony.

Her empathy was praised, yet her strategic insights were sometimes overlooked. Her emotional steadiness was relied upon, yet she was excluded from certain decision-making spaces where her perspective was needed most.

This invisible labour was essential to the mission's functioning, yet it remained undocumented, unmeasured, and unacknowledged.

Mariana carried it anyway.

The Internal Cost of Emotional Containment

Representation demands emotional resilience, but resilience has a cost. Mariana felt it in the quiet moments, the heaviness she carried home, the private tears she shed after a difficult case, the emotional distance she sometimes needed to maintain as self-protection.

She confronted her own doubts:
Am I doing enough?
Am I strong enough?
Am I failing them?

She silenced the internal voice that questioned her adequacy. She cultivated an inner steadiness that did not depend on external validation. This resilience became her shield, not hard, but firm; not cold, but grounded.

Yet the toll accumulated. Each crisis left a subtle imprint. Each emotionally charged interaction added weight. Each moment of being underestimated left a mark.

Still, she persisted.

Emotional Labour as Leadership

Despite the burden, emotional labour deepened Mariana's leadership. It sharpened her discernment, strengthened her empathy, and refined her ability to navigate complexity with grace. She learned to respond to crises with clarity, to hold space for others without losing herself, and to lead with compassion without compromising authority.

Her emotional steadiness became a quiet form of leadership, one that did not seek recognition but shaped the culture of her mission. Colleagues trusted her. Citizens relied on her. Headquarters valued her clarity.

Through emotional labour, a diplomat became not only a representative of her nation but a steward of human experience.

Lesson Learnt

Mariana's experience in Pretoria demonstrates that emotional labour is not merely an ancillary aspect of diplomacy; rather, it constitutes one of its most defining and challenging dimensions. She recognises that representing a nation requires more than procedural proficiency; it demands the ability to manage others' emotions with composure, empathy, and restraint. She finds that emotional containment exemplifies a form of leadership.

The capacity to maintain composure while absorbing the distress of citizens, the impatience of headquarters, and the limitations of local systems becomes a subtle demonstration of strength.

Most profoundly, she learns that emotional labour shapes her identity as a diplomat. It deepens her empathy, sharpens her judgement, and strengthens her resilience. Yet it also leaves an imprint of private exhaustion, unspoken heaviness, and quiet moments when she must gather herself before continuing.

Ultimately, Mariana's journey teaches her that representation is not merely political; it is deeply human. Through this unseen, unrecorded, yet indispensable labour, she embodies the truth that diplomacy is not only the management of interests but also the stewardship of human experience.

CHAPTER ELEVEN

Unspoken Obligations: The Tacit Expectations Embedded in Diplomatic Duties

The Expectations

Copenhagen received First Secretary Amara Mensah with a composed demeanour so refined that it nearly concealed the underlying pressure. She arrived with an exemplary professional record; however, her presence was not merely an announcement of her credentials, but also a set of unspoken assumptions. She was the youngest officer on the team and the sole Black woman within the building. She sensed the silent scrutiny before uttering a single word. Colleagues observed to determine whether she would integrate seamlessly, adapt, or demonstrate her competence.

The expectations were unstated yet unmistakable, conveyed through pauses, glances, and the subtle way individuals awaited her first briefing. Her initial high-level meeting demonstrated the significance of these assumptions.

A senior official unexpectedly addressed her, inquiring, "What does your delegation think?"

This was a subtle yet deliberate test.

Amara took a deep breath, maintaining composure and confidence, and articulated her position with clarity, nuance, and calm authority.

The atmosphere in the room shifted subtly, like a tide turning before anyone noticed. Subsequently, a colleague remarked, "You handled that well," and beneath the compliment, she discerned the unspoken message: we were uncertain you would succeed. Walking home through the cold Danish air, she realised that the expectations she carried were not written anywhere, yet they shaped her experience with undeniable force.

The Burden of Being Exceptional

Unspoken expectations constitute some of the most formidable pressures encountered by female diplomats. They shape perceptions, evaluations, and opportunities well before any spoken interaction occurs. For Amara, the burden initially manifested as the expectation to surpass merely competent performance; she was required to demonstrate exceptional skill. To achieve parity, she was compelled to exert twice the effort, anticipate questions, proactively prepare for potential challenges, and consistently deliver impeccable results. Her margin for error was exceedingly limited, and her allowance for doubt was minimal. Even when her qualifications were evident, she often felt the necessity to repeatedly justify her presence.

This expectation dictated her daily routine. She arrived earlier than her colleagues, prepared more diligently, and rehearsed her interventions with utmost meticulousness. She predicted reactions before they occurred and continually refined her tone, phrasing, and posture.

She bore the continuous burden of proving herself, cognizant that any misstep would be perceived not merely as an individual error but as an affirmation of an unspoken assumption.

The Performance of Voice and Presence

Unspoken expectations shaped not only Amara's professional conduct but also her way of expressing herself. She quickly realised that her words would be scrutinised more closely than those of her colleagues. She needed to balance assertiveness with diplomacy, confidence with humility, and clarity with restraint. A decisive tone risked being perceived as harsh. A quiet moment risked being interpreted as uncertainty. A firm stance risked being seen as inflexible. Her tone became a performance, not out of insincerity but out of necessity, carefully crafted to avoid misinterpretation.

Her presence carried similar weight. She was required to project confidence even when uncertain, maintain composure despite frustration, and appear unaffected by stinging remarks or assumptions that undermined her. Her demeanour became an integral part of her professional armour, refined and steady, serving as a shield against the subtle biases that remained beneath the surface. She learned to read the room with heightened sensitivity, adjusting her tone and posture to navigate expectations that, although unspoken, were universally acknowledged and enforced.

Gendered Expectations

For the female diplomat, unspoken expectations are intensified by gender. Amara felt this acutely. She was expected to be nurturing without being emotional, assertive without being aggressive, and competent without overshadowing others. Stereotypes shaped how her actions were interpreted. A firm tone could be misread as abrasive. A moment of vulnerability could be seen as a weakness. Ambition could be misconstrued as arrogance.

These expectations significantly influenced her daily experiences more profoundly than any formal assessment. Additionally, she assumed the role of informal mediator, the individual colleagues approached to de-escalate tensions, the person distressed citizens sought out, and the one anticipated to facilitate difficult conversations. This emotional labour was vital to the mission's operation; however, it remained unrecorded and unrecognised. Nevertheless, she bore this burden, cognizant that her stability was relied upon even when her strategic insights were disregarded.

The Internal Battle: Self-Imbibed Expectations

The internal burden was equally significant. Amara carried her own hopes, fears, and aspirations. She wished to honour the sacrifices that facilitated her journey. She aimed to make her family proud. She sought to open doors for those who would follow. She endeavoured to demonstrate, to herself and to others, that she belonged. These internal expectations served as motivation, yet they also posed overwhelming challenges. She experienced pressure to maintain perfection, to remain unwavering, and to conceal fatigue. She rehearsed responses, anticipated reactions, and prepared meticulously for every engagement.

However, the burden was not solely a weight; it also acted as a catalyst. It heightened her awareness, fortified her resilience, and deepened her understanding of herself and her purpose. Through these pressures, she evolved into a diplomat not only through formal training but also through endurance. She learned to navigate complexity with composure, respond to pressure with clarity, and transcend assumptions with quiet confidence.

The Quiet Strength That Redefines the Institution

Still, the burden accumulated. It appeared in moments she could not share, in the fatigue she carried in silence, in the pressure to be perfect, and in the emotional labour she performed without acknowledgement. And yet, she persisted. She persisted because she recognised the significance of her presence. She persisted because her achievements expanded the boundaries of what was possible. She persisted because she believed in diplomacy, in service, and in the calling that brought her here.

In the end, the weight of unspoken expectations did not diminish her. It revealed her. It shaped her into a diplomat who led with purpose, navigated complexity with wisdom, and represented her nation with dignity. Through her perseverance, she redefined the expectations placed upon her, creating a future in which women enter the room unburdened by the weight she once carried alone.

Lesson Learnt

Amara's journey in Copenhagen reveals that the most influential forces shaping a diplomat's experience frequently remain unacknowledged. She recognises that unspoken expectations, subtle yet pervasive, can influence her confidence, opportunities, and perceptions of her presence long before she articulates herself. She finds that managing these expectations necessitates a cultivated inner composure. Her capacity to anticipate assumptions, respond with clarity rather than defensiveness, and sustain dignity amidst scepticism exemplifies a discreet form of leadership.

Most profoundly, she learns that unspoken expectations do not merely test her; they shape her. They sharpen her discernment, deepen her resilience, and strengthen her sense of purpose. Her presence becomes an act of transformation, expanding what is possible and creating pathways for those who will follow.

Ultimately, Amara's experience teaches her that the weight of unspoken expectations is not a burden she bears in vain. It becomes evidence of her capacity to lead with wisdom, endure with dignity, and redefine the very standards she was once expected to meet. Through her perseverance, she turns the unspoken into the undeniable: she belongs, she contributes, and she reshapes the institution simply by standing firmly as who she is.

CHAPTER TWELVE

Custodianship of National Narrative: The Diplomat as Cultural Archivist

The Sacred Weight of Carrying a Nation's Story

There is a crucial yet often overlooked role that female diplomats fulfil: they become custodians of their nation's narrative. Unlike mere narrators of slogans or polished myths, they bear witness to the truth, the essence of their people, their survivals, aspirations, and the resolutions to prevent history from repeating itself. This narrative manifests through her voice, posture, and presence. It is expressed in her manner of listening, negotiating, and responding to provocations. Moreover, she sustains this narrative by refusing to allow her nation to be reduced to stereotypes or mere statistics. This profound duty is not merely ceremonial but is a lived experience.

Ambassador Farida Suleiman understood this responsibility intimately. At a regional summit in Addis Ababa, she found herself in a tense exchange with a delegation that repeatedly misrepresented her country's history. They described her nation as fragile, unstable, and perpetually dependent, with the confidence of those who had never walked her streets, met her people, or understood the resilience woven into her homeland. Farida listened, not with anger but with clarity. When it was her turn to speak, she did not recite policy. She told a story. She spoke of the women who rebuilt communities after conflict, the farmers who fed entire regions during drought, the young innovators who created solutions despite limited resources, the elders who preserved wisdom across generations, and the dignity her people carried even in hardship.

The room shifted, not because she argued, but because she revealed. She reminded them that nations are not headlines. They are living beings, layered, courageous, and complex. Her story did not erase her nation's challenges. It contextualised them. It dignified them. It reframed them.

The Preparation Behind the Voice

This sacred work does not commence within conference rooms. Instead, it originates in the tranquil spaces where she prepares herself to bear a narrative greater than her individual existence. Farida examined her nation's history not merely as an academic pursuit but as an inheritance. She familiarised herself with its wounds, triumphs, and contradictions. She sought out the narratives that were silenced, distorted, or left untold. She assimilated the cultural rhythms, unspoken codes, and collective memories that influenced her people's worldview.

She understood that every nation carries two narratives: the one it presents to the world and the one the world tells about it. Her task was to reconcile them without compromising her people's identity. She had to correct misconceptions without defensiveness, assert truths without hostility, and illuminate complexities without apology. This work demanded emotional intelligence, historical awareness, and cultural fluency. It required communicating with authority without aggression, educating without condescension, and challenging without alienating. *Farida became a guardian of context, understanding that diplomacy without context is performative, but diplomacy rooted in understanding reveals truth.*

Confronting Misrepresentation with Courage

To articulate the truth about her nation is to confront narratives that diminish it. Farida encountered stereotypes embedded in policy, assumptions repeated so often they were mistaken for fact, and commentary delivered with the confidence of distance rather than of experience. She had to speak for her nation in rooms where it was absent. She had to correct narratives that reduced her country to its most tragic moments or its most convenient caricatures.

This was not easy work. It was emotional, intellectual, political, and profoundly human. To hold a nation's story is to hold its dignity. Farida understood that every time she spoke, she was not merely offering information; she was restoring balance. She was reclaiming agency. She was ensuring that her people were not defined by others' narrow imaginations.

Her courage was not loud. It was steady. It was rooted in truth.

The Inward Burden of Representation

This sacred duty was not only external but also internal. Farida needed to uphold her nation's narrative without allowing it to consume her. She bore the responsibility of representing her people while preserving her individuality. She was tasked with embodying her people's interests without succumbing to the weight of their expectations. She had to distinguish her personal worth from her nation's reputation.

She was required to maintain a sense of pride without descending into perfectionism. Moreover, she needed to speak truthfully without believing she alone had to safeguard it.

This balance was delicate. It was learned through experience, mistakes, and moments of doubt and revelation. There were days when the burden felt heavy, the responsibility overwhelming, and the expectations impossible to meet. Yet she persisted. She persisted because she understood that narratives shape policy, perception, and possibility. She recognised that change is driven not only by data but also by stories that challenge assumptions, restore nuance, and expand the imagination.

The Diplomat as Cultural Archivist

Farida's persistence was rooted in a calling that transcended her professional duties, a vocation to ensure her nation's story was acknowledged, understood, and remembered with dignity. She became a living testament to her people's resilience, a quiet historian of their courage, and a diplomat who not only represented her nation but also revealed its essence.

Through her work, she ensured that her country's narrative was preserved, unmarred, and esteemed, carried forward with honour, clarity, and integrity. She recognised that the diplomat, as a cultural archivist, is not solely a representative of the state but also a guardian of identity. She held memory in one hand and possibility in the other, bridging the divide between the external perception of her nation and the true identity of her people. This is the sacred work. This is the burden.
This is the gift.

And because of her, the world saw her nation not through assumption, but through truth, a truth she carried with dignity, courage, and reverence into every room she entered.

Lesson Learnt

Farida's experience in Addis Ababa illustrates that the most effective instrument for a diplomat is not persuasion but truth, truth communicated with clarity, dignity, and an acute awareness of historical context. She recognises that safeguarding her nation's narrative is not an act of defensiveness but of restoration; it ensures that her people are acknowledged in their entirety, rather than through distortions, distance, or stereotypes. She comes to understand that managing her nation's narrative requires meticulous preparation. To advocate effectively for her country, she must first attain a comprehensive understanding of it, including its wounds, triumphs, silences, and complexities.

This knowledge becomes her armour, her guide, and her authority. Through this, she acknowledges that diplomacy rooted in cultural memory is resilient and cannot be easily dismissed. Most importantly, she appreciates that bearing her nation's story is both an honour and a burden; it demands courage to confront misrepresentation, discipline to maintain balance, and humility to accept that she is a conduit for a truth greater than herself.

Nonetheless, it grants her a profound sense of purpose: the understanding that her presence can reshape perceptions, restore dignity, and foster understanding.

Ultimately, Farida's journey teaches her that the diplomat-as-cultural-archivist is not merely a state representative but a guardian of identity. Through her voice, clarity, and courage, she ensures that her nation's story is not lost, diminished, or distorted, but carried forward with honour, truth, and reverence.

CHAPTER THIRTEEN

Reclaiming Narrative Authority: Voice, Agency, and Diplomatic Expression

The Silence

Rabat received Counsellor Leïla Benyoussef in an atmosphere of warmth that evoked antiquity, like a sun that illuminated everything except those aspects of herself she had learned to suppress. Her posting in Stockholm marked her inaugural assignment outside the regional sphere, characterised by a commitment to efficiency, politeness, and a discreet hierarchy that manifested through subtle cues. During her initial month, she discerned a recurring pattern that remained unspoken yet influenced every interaction. When she contributed, colleagues expressed acknowledgement but proceeded without further engagement. When she offered insights, others echoed them, and they were subsequently taken seriously. When she voiced concerns, they were 'noted" and seldom addressed. Although no one explicitly instructed her to remain silent, the environment implicitly instructed her to diminish her presence.

Her two fundamental skills, strategic articulation and inner stability, became her essential resources. She learned to interpret pauses, glances, and subtle shifts that indicated when her presence was being minimised. She perceived the silent erasure, the delicate sidelining, and the unspoken expectation that she should wait her turn, soften her tone, or defer to others. The silence she bore was not voluntary; it was imposed.

Moments in her career

The turning point came during a negotiation on migration policy. Leïla had prepared the brief, drafted the talking points, and anticipated every counterargument. Yet when the meeting began, her head of mission gestured for another colleague to speak in her place. The familiar tightening in her chest returned, the quiet erasure, the subtle dismissal of her expertise. But this time, she inhaled deeply, lifted her chin, and said calmly, "Ambassador, if I may, I wrote the analysis. I want to present it."

The room paused, not in resistance but in surprise. She spoke clearly, measuredly, grounded in her own authority. Her voice did not tremble. Her presence did not waver. When she finished, the delegation across the table said, "Thank you. That was the most coherent framing we have heard today." As they left, her head of mission murmured, "You should speak more frequently." She smiled, not out of gratitude but recognition. She had not found her voice that day. She had reclaimed it.

The Slow Return to Her Own Truth

Reclaiming one's voice is one of the most profound acts of self-restoration a female diplomat undertakes. It is not loud or dramatic. It is a gradual return to her truth, a truth often muted by institutions, cultures, and the subtle pressures of diplomacy. The process begins with acknowledging the silence she did not choose, the silence imposed through interruptions, dismissals, assumptions, and the quiet minimisation of her contributions.

Leïla began to notice the moments when she edited herself, hesitated before speaking, or swallowed her insight because she anticipated resistance. She recognised the internal voice that whispered, Wait. Not now. Not you. And she began to challenge it. Reclaiming her voice required courage, not the kind that announces itself, but the quiet determination that says, I deserve to be heard.

She learned to speak even when her voice wavered, to assert her expertise despite scepticism, and to refuse to fade into the background of her own career. Her voice became an instrument she had to retune continually. She rediscovered her tone, resolute but not severe, clear but not defensive, confident but not performative.

Reclaiming Authority Through Presence

Reclaiming her voice also meant regaining her authority. Leïla began speaking earlier in meetings, no longer waiting for permission. She challenged assumptions with clarity rather than hesitation. She posed questions that shifted the dynamics of the room. She articulated ideas that influenced decision-making. She occupied space, not aggressively, but with grounded confidence.

Reclaiming her voice was not solely about speech; it also concerned recognition. It was an insistence that her contributions be acknowledged, her expertise valued, and her presence respected. It was a refusal to accept the misconception that silence equates to agreement or that quietude signifies a lack of insight. She recognised that her voice was not merely sound; it represented agency. It was the expression of her judgment, her experience, her identity. Each time she used it, she reclaimed a part of herself that had been quietly taken.

The Collective Strength Behind Her Voice

Reclaiming her voice was not a solitary act. It was shaped by mentors who encouraged her, colleagues who amplified her, and allies who created space for her. It was strengthened by the women who came before her and those who stood beside her. It was sustained by the understanding that her voice contributed to a collective chorus reshaping diplomacy.

Yet the journey continued. There were moments of hesitation, when the room felt too heavy, when silence seemed safer. But each time she spoke authentically, she strengthened her voice.

Each time she asserted her presence, she expanded the boundaries of inclusion. Each time she refused to diminish herself, she reclaimed her identity.

The Boundaries That Protect Her Voice

Reclaiming her voice also meant reclaiming her boundaries. Leïla learned to say no without guilt. She refused to shoulder emotional labour that was not hers. She protected her time, energy, and clarity. She recognised that her voice was not only what she said; it was also what she refused to accept. In doing so, she reclaimed her authority.

For the female diplomat, her voice is not an accessory to her work. It is the instrument through which she shapes the world.

Lesson Learnt

Leïla's experience in Stockholm reveals that reclaiming one's voice is not an act of defiance but an act of alignment, a return to the truth she had been taught to mute. She recognises that silence can be enforced without a single word, through subtle dismissals, quiet erasures, and invisible pressures that determine who is heard and who is overlooked. Reclaiming her voice becomes an act of self-restoration, a means of honouring her expertise, her presence, and her right to influence the spaces she inhabits.

She comes to understand that voice is not merely sound; it embodies agency. It signifies the courage to speak when silence appears the easier option, the discipline to articulate the truth without apology, and the wisdom to recognise that her insights have value even if others fail to acknowledge them. Through this realisation, she understands that reclaiming her voice is inherently linked to reclaiming her authority.

Most significantly, she learns that her voice is not exclusively hers. Each time she articulates with clarity, she paves the way for others. Each refusal to be diminished challenges the structures that silence women's voices. Each assertion of her presence contributes to reshaping the culture of diplomacy itself.

Ultimately, Leïla's journey teaches that reclaiming her voice is not a one-off act but a continuous practice, a deliberate, ongoing choice of truth over fear, presence over erasure, and agency over silence. Through her voice, she becomes not merely a diplomat but also a guardian of her own narrative, shaping the world with clarity, courage, and unwavering authenticity.

CHAPTER FOURTEEN

The Invisible Hand That Unites: Dual Allegiance and the Unseen Choreography

Two Worlds, One Woman

Shanghai in winter has a way of slowing the world. Breath becomes mist, footsteps soften under frost, and the city settles into a ceremonial quiet. But for Consul General Odinaso Nwaibe, that morning offered no such stillness. At 6:47 a.m., her secure line rang: a crisis had erupted in a neighbouring region, and the minister required a briefing at exactly 8:00 a.m. At 6:49 a.m., her teenage daughter sent a frantic message: she had forgotten her science project at home, and it was due that morning. Two worlds. Two urgencies. One woman.

Odinaso made her decision not because she had time, but because she had mastered the impossible. She called her driver, retrieved the project from the dining table, and stepped into the icy morning. At 7:32 a.m., she delivered the project to the school. Her daughter hugged her tightly, whispering gratitude into her coat. By 7:58 a.m., she was in her office, hair damp with snow, documents spread before her, her voice steady as she briefed the minister on the unfolding crisis. No one on the call knew she had just saved her daughter's day. No one realised she had managed two crises, one global, one intimate, with equal precision.

This is the unseen labour of the female diplomat: holding her family together while holding her nation together. She does not choose between the two. She carries both with elegance, exhaustion, love, and discipline.

The Choreography Beneath Her Calm

Her life is not a balancing act; it is a choreography. The invisible hand that unites is not metaphorical. It is lived. It is the force that binds the disparate threads of her life without allowing any of them to snap. Her professional responsibilities extend far beyond conference rooms and negotiation halls. They live in the margins, early mornings, late nights, and the quiet spaces between official duties, where she becomes the cohesive force that keeps everything from falling apart. The institution sees her title. The world sees her flag. But her family sees the woman who remembers birthdays, school projects, medical appointments, and the emotional temperature of her home. She is the quiet principle of cohesion, the one who prevents disintegration.

Her day begins long before the first meeting. She wakes with an internal checklist, not of tasks but of people. Who needs reassurance today? Which colleague is carrying unspoken tension? What cultural nuance must she navigate? What need must she anticipate? What crisis might erupt without warning? She moves through her morning with a precision that appears effortless from the outside. She responds to messages while packing lunchboxes. She reviews briefs while checking on ageing parents. She rehearses talking points while reminding her children to wear their coats. Her life is a series of intertwined responsibilities, none of which she can abandon. Yet she carries them with a composure that conceals their weight.

The Emotional Core of Her Leadership

The invisible force that unites her efforts is not only logistical; it is emotional.

She is the one who calms her team during tense moments, reassures distressed citizens, absorbs colleagues' anxieties, mediates conflicts discreetly, softens institutional rigidity, and infuses humanity into spaces that often overlook it. She becomes the emotional anchor of her mission, not because her job description demands it, but because she understands that diplomacy is ultimately about people. And people require steadiness. People require warmth. People require someone who can bear the emotional weight of the moment without collapsing under it.

Her emotional labour is not visible in official reports, yet it shapes the culture of her mission. It stabilises her team. It strengthens her institution. It humanises her work. She becomes the quiet centre that holds everything together.

The Dual Allegiance She Carries Alone

The female diplomat bears a dual allegiance that is noble yet demanding. She has sworn an oath to her nation and holds an unspoken commitment to her family. Both rely on her presence, strength, and discernment. Yet neither fully understands the other's demands. Her country sees her as a representative; her family sees her as irreplaceable. She stands between two worlds that rarely acknowledge each other, managing both with a grace that masks the strain beneath.

Her sacrifices are seldom visible. They are discreet, persistent, and cumulative. She forfeits sleep to complete reports, sacrifices rest to comfort a child, gives up weekends for official engagements, and sets aside personal desires to uphold national responsibilities. She draws on emotional reserves to carry burdens that are not her own. These sacrifices do not appear in performance evaluations.

They do not earn medals. They are not photographed or celebrated. Yet they form the foundation on which her world is built.

The Quiet Leadership That Holds the Centre

The unseen force that unites is also a form of leadership, subtle, steady, and transformative. She leads by anticipating needs before they are voiced, fostering harmony in tense situations, providing clarity in moments of confusion, stabilising her team during periods of uncertainty, and maintaining the emotional core of her mission. This leadership is not loud or performative. It is quiet, consistent, profoundly human. It shapes institutions not through declarations but through presence.

There are moments when the burden feels heavy, when she sits in her car after a long day and lets silence wash over her, when she closes her office door and lets out the breath she has held for hours, when she wonders how long she can sustain everything, when she feels the solitude of being the one everyone depends on.

But even in these moments, she does not break. She bends, she stretches, she recalibrates, but she does not break.

Her strength is not in being invulnerable. Her strength is in continuing, even when no one sees the effort it takes.

The Legacy Woven Through Her Presence

The invisible hand that unites is not only about survival; it is about legacy. Her children grow up watching a woman who leads with dignity. Her colleagues learn from her steadiness. Her presence strengthens her mission. Her nation is represented with compassion because she embodies both heart and discipline. She shapes the next generation not through speeches but by setting an example.

Her legacy is not ostentatious.

It is not theatrical.

It is not carved in monuments. Instead, it is embedded in the lives she influences, the environments she stabilises, and the worlds she sustains. She comes to realise a profound truth: her responsibilities are not solely defined by her actions but also by the person she becomes. She evolves into the unseen force that holds the core together, the individual who preserves the essential elements, and the one who refuses to allow chaos to take root.

She embodies rhythm.

She embodies stability.

She embodies continuity.

She reveals an often-overlooked truth about diplomacy: nations are sustained not only by treaties and negotiations but also by the quiet, unacknowledged labour of those who prevent the world from falling apart.

Lessons Learnt

Consul General Odinaso Nwaibe's story reveals that the female diplomat's greatest strength lies not in her public achievements but in the unseen choreography that sustains both her family and her nation.

The chapter teaches that dual allegiance is not a flaw in her design but a defining feature of her leadership. She learns that her life is not a balancing act but a continuous negotiation between two worlds that demand her presence, her steadiness, and her emotional intelligence. Her ability to move seamlessly between global crises and intimate responsibilities is not accidental; it is a discipline shaped by love, duty, and resilience.

The shows that the invisible labour she performs, the emotional anchoring, the quiet mediation, the anticipation of needs, the stabilising presence she brings into every room, is a form of leadership that rarely receives recognition. Her institution sees her title, but her family sees her humanity. Her colleagues see her composure, but only she feels the weight beneath it. She learns that her sacrifices, though unseen, are foundational: they hold her mission together, sustain her home, and shape the emotional climate of her work.

Ultimately, she discovers that the invisible hand that unites is not a metaphor but a lived truth.

Her leadership is not loud or performative; it is quiet, consistent, and profoundly human.

She realises that her legacy is not measured by the speeches she delivers or the treaties she negotiates, but by the lives she steadies, the environments she strengthens, and the worlds she sustains.

In embracing her dual allegiance, she becomes the unseen force that holds the centre, the embodiment of rhythm, stability, and continuity. And in this truth, she finds her strength: not in being invulnerable, but in being the woman who refuses to let anything fall apart.

PART II

THE EMOTIONAL AND PSYCHOLOGICAL BURDENS OF REPRESENTATION

"Her silence is not absence; it is a strategy."- Kemi.

Architectural Prelude

Part II delineates the diplomat's progression beyond mere identity formation into the more intricate domain of representation, where her presence assumes a political dimension; her silence is subjected to interpretation; her voice is subject to contention; and her emotional landscape becomes an integral component of her professional arsenal. These chapters examine the significance she carries, not because of her title, but because of her presence in spaces that have historically been non-neutral.

Part II uncovers the concealed labour inherent in diplomacy: the emotional toll of managing others' fears, the unspoken expectations that influence her conduct, the internal negotiations necessary for her well-being, and the ongoing adjustments required to uphold her dignity in environments that challenge her boundaries.

This section critically analyses the burdens not documented in job descriptions, the psychological pressures, the cultural contradictions, the demands for impeccable performance, and the silent resilience essential to reclaiming her voice, authority, and narrative.

Part II marks the point where the diplomat transcends the role of a mere representative of the state. She assumes the responsibilities of custodian of her nation's story, steward of her personal truth, and the discreet architect of her endurance.

CHAPTER FIFTEEN

The Quiet Power of Reinvention: Adaptation as Diplomatic Survival

The Discipline of Becoming

Reinvention is not a luxury for the female diplomat; it is a survival skill, a quiet discipline she wears like a second skin, a capacity she draws on whenever the ground beneath her shifts. She reinvents herself with each new posting, each cultural landscape, each moment when she is underestimated and then exceeds expectations. Reinvention is not an event in her life; it is the rhythm that defines it.

For First Secretary Hana Kim, that rhythm began the moment she stepped into Jakarta's monsoon-soaked air. The humidity clung to her skin like a second atmosphere, thick and unrelenting. She had been trained in trade policy, negotiation forums, tariff disputes, and economic frameworks.

That was her world.

But within months, she was reassigned to an entirely different field: climate negotiations. A senior colleague had fallen ill. A regional summit was approaching. The mission needed someone to step in. The responsibility landed on her desk with the quiet inevitability that defines diplomatic life. She had never studied climate science. She had never drafted a climate brief. She had never attended a climate summit.

Yet the moment required her to become something she had never been.

The Night Work of Reinvention

Instead of shrinking, Hana reinvented herself. She dedicated her nights to studying technical reports, her apartment lit by the gentle glow of a desk lamp as tropical rain tap-danced against the windows. She attended workshops incognito, sitting in the back row, learning about carbon markets, adaptation strategies, and emission pathways. She posed questions confidently, refusing to let pride impede her progress. She forged discreet alliances with researchers, experts, and regional partners eager to share their insights. Through discipline, humility, and unwavering confidence that she could meet the moment, she transformed from a novice into an authority.

Six months later, she delivered a speech at a regional summit that was cited in three national newspapers. A senior diplomat approached her and remarked, “I did not realise you were a climate expert.” She smiled, not with arrogance, but with the composed certainty of someone who had reorganised herself internally. “I was not,” she replied. “I became one.”

For the female diplomat, reinvention does not entail altering identity. It signifies the expansion of self while preserving core essence. She does not await authorisation to evolve. She evolves because the world requires it, and because she recognises that her potential surpasses others’ expectations.

The Adaptation That Sustains Her

The necessity of reinvention begins with recognising that her environment is in constant flux. Political landscapes shift, alliances realign, emergencies erupt without warning, and cultural expectations differ across postings. She understands that rigidity is a liability; adaptability becomes her most valuable asset. Reinvention is her strategy for continuity and success.

She redefines herself intellectually, emotionally, and professionally. She learns new languages, not only spoken ones but also cultural languages: the language of silence in East Asia, the language of hospitality in the Middle East, the language of hierarchy in Europe, and the language of warmth in Latin America. She studies the unspoken rules of each society she enters, adjusting her tone, pace, and presence accordingly. She becomes adept at reading nuance, context, and the subtle shifts that determine whether negotiations succeed or fail.

Reinvention requires emotional resilience. She must detach without becoming indifferent, empathise without becoming overwhelmed, and care deeply without losing herself. She rebuilds her support networks with each move, forming new friendships, establishing new routines, and finding new anchors. She learns to let go of her past without erasing it. Reinvention demands that she carry her history lightly while embracing her present fully.

The Solitude of Becoming

There is a solitude within reinvention that few understand. Each new assignment requires her to dismantle parts of her life and rebuild them in unfamiliar surroundings. She must find new grocery stores, doctors, and schools for her children. She must learn which roads flood in the monsoon season, which neighbourhoods are safe at night, and which gestures convey respect. She must learn to be authentic in a place where she is still a stranger. Reinvention is not glamorous. It is subtle, demanding, and often invisible.

Yet reinvention is profoundly empowering. It enables her to integrate into diverse environments, adapt to new social rhythms, and confront challenges she has never faced. It builds resilience, helping her recover from setbacks. Reinvention proves she is not confined by her past roles or limitations. She is defined by her capacity for growth. Reinvention becomes her quiet counterargument to underestimation. She is told she is too young, too gentle, too emotional, too inexperienced. She hears these doubts, spoken and unspoken. But instead of internalising them, she turns them into fuel. She reconstructs herself not to contradict others, but to affirm her own worth.

The Courage and Humility of Transformation

Reinvention requires humility, the humility to say, "I do not know," not as an admission of inadequacy but as an invitation to learn. She asks questions, seeks guidance, and adopts a learner's posture even when she is expected to be the expert. Humility becomes her strength, enabling transformation. Reinvention also demands courage, the courage to step into roles she did not anticipate, to take on responsibilities she did not seek, and to trust her capacity even when the future is unclear. Courage is not the absence of fear; it is the decision to move forward despite it.

The quiet power of reinvention lies in discipline. It is not spontaneous; it is intentional. It requires late nights, early mornings, and the unglamorous labour of learning. It requires patience, consistency, and the willingness to persist even when progress feels slow.

Reinvention is not a spark; it is a sustained flame.

The Leadership Born from Reinvention

Reinvention shapes her leadership. She leads not through rigidity but through adaptability. Her leadership is guided not by ego but by curiosity. It is defined not by certainty but by a willingness to learn. Her leadership becomes dynamic, responsive, and grounded in the understanding that growth is continuous. Her reinvention becomes a gift to others. Younger diplomats observe her evolution and realise they can do the same. Colleagues see her step beyond her comfort zone and find the courage to follow suit. Her reinvention serves as mentorship, quiet, powerful, and transformative.

Reinvention also functions as a form of self-preservation. Diplomacy can be unforgiving, demanding, and emotionally draining. Reinvention sustains her within the profession. It nurtures her curiosity, engagement, and sense of purpose. Without reinvention, stagnation would occur. With it, she is able to flourish. She understands that reinvention is not a departure from her identity; it is a return to her potential. She reinvents herself not to escape who she is, but to become more fully who she was always meant to be.

Lesson Learnt

Hana's journey in Jakarta reveals that reinvention is not a reaction to crisis but a disciplined practice of growth. She learns that adaptability is not instability but strength, the capacity to evolve without losing her essence. Reinvention becomes her strategy for navigating uncertainty, broadening her expertise, and stepping into roles she never imagined.

She discovers that humility and courage are the twin engines of transformation. Humility allows her to say, “I do not know,” while courage allows her to say, “But I can learn.” Each reinvention strengthens her leadership, deepens her resilience, and expands her capacity. Ultimately, Hana discovers that reinvention is the quiet power that sustains her, a discipline of becoming that enables her to meet the world not with fear, but with readiness. Through reinvention, she becomes not only a diplomat but a dynamic, evolving force shaped by purpose, curiosity, and unwavering determination.

CHAPTER SIXTEEN

The Cost of Emotional Containment: The Battle Within

The Quiet War

There is a clandestine struggle that the female diplomat endures, an internal conflict unseen by observers, occurring not within negotiation chambers or policy briefings but within the silent recesses of her own mind. This is the struggle to maintain her humanity amidst a profession that frequently demands she become a symbol: a representative of national interests, a steady voice during crises, and a composed presence amid chaos. Her competence, poise, and discipline are apparent to the external world; however, the emotional sacrifices required to sustain such composure, even as her inner self trembles, remain unacknowledged.

Deputy Ambassador Sofia Alvarez understood this struggle intimately. When she arrived in Warsaw, she was known for her meticulousness and emotional steadiness. She had managed political crises across South America, mediated disputes in multilateral forums, and represented her nation during periods of national mourning. *Yet nothing prepared her for the Polish winter, a cold that seeped into her bones and lingered like a shadow.*

The geopolitical climate was tense.

The embassy was understaffed. Demands were relentless. Each day brought a new crisis: a detained citizen, a diplomatic misunderstanding, a security alert, a late-night call from the capital demanding immediate clarification.

Sofia managed each situation with the calm professionalism her role necessitated. She composed formal statements, coordinated official responses, reassured concerned families, and briefed her ambassador, demonstrating a composed demeanour indicative of mastery over emotional regulation. However, in the evenings, upon returning to her residence, the pervasive silence became oppressive. She would sit on the edge of her bed, still dressed in her coat, unable to move for several minutes. This was not solely fatigue; it was the gradual erosion of her humanity and the depletion of emotional reserves that remained perpetually unrefilled.

The Weight of Perpetual Composure

The struggle to preserve her humanity begins with the expectation that she must remain perpetually composed. She is not permitted to cry in meetings, raise her voice, show frustration, reveal fear, or appear overwhelmed. She must keep her personal life from intruding on her professional responsibilities. She is expected to be the calm in every storm, the steady hand in every crisis, the voice of reason when others falter.

And so, she learns to suppress her emotions, conceal them behind a veneer of professionalism, and carry them silently until they become unbearable. But the human heart is not designed for suppression. It requires release, tenderness, and vulnerability. It needs moments of rest and reassurance, not the perpetual burden of emotional restraint. The female diplomat rarely encounters these moments. She is the one others seek, rely on, and look to for strength.

She cultivates resilience not because she is invulnerable, but because she sees no alternative.

The Grief She Cannot Show

The struggle for her humanity manifests in her relationship with grief. She may lose a loved one while stationed thousands of miles away, unable to return home in time for the funeral. She may receive devastating news minutes before a high-level meeting, compelled to steady her voice and proceed as if nothing has occurred. She may carry heartbreak into negotiation rooms, her personal suffering concealed beneath diplomatic language. She may feel profoundly lonely in her apartment at night, yet present the following morning with a smile sufficiently convincing to reassure others.

Diplomacy does not pause for her humanity; consequently, she adapts by dividing herself into the woman who feels and the diplomat who performs. However, this division is never flawless. Emotional remnants accumulate, settling in the corners of her life like dust she has no opportunity to sweep away.

The Moral Weight She Must Carry

The struggle to preserve her humanity also manifests in the moral dilemmas she is compelled to confront. There are instances in which her personal values conflict with national directives, in which her conscience urges her toward a particular course of action while her official instructions prescribe another. She must represent positions with which she may not fully concur, defend decisions she did not personally make, and uphold policies she did not formulate.

A female diplomat is required to speak with unwavering conviction, even when her innermost feelings are conflicted.

Furthermore, she must suppress the aspects of herself that yearn to question, challenge, or resist. In doing so, she risks losing parts of her identity. Yet she fights to retain her humanity through small, deliberate acts.

She remembers the names of the mission's support staff.

She checks on colleagues who seem withdrawn.

She comforts distressed citizens with warmth that goes beyond protocol. She writes to her family late at night, anchoring herself to a world beyond her responsibilities.

She finds moments of tenderness, such as a cup of tea at dawn, a walk through a quiet park, or a phone call with a friend who sees her beyond her title.

These moments become her lifeline.

The Moment.

Sofia found her lifeline one evening at a small community concert in Warsaw. A local partner had invited her, and she almost declined, overwhelmed by her duties. Yet something quiet within urged her to go. The concert took place in a modest auditorium filled with families, students, and elderly couples. When the music began, something within her released. The melodies were simple, honest, and warm. Tears welled in her eyes, not from sorrow but from recognition. She realised she had been living in survival mode, functioning without feeling, performing without presence. That evening, she allowed herself to breathe.

The Battle to Remain Whole

The struggle to preserve her humanity is not a single victory; it is a continuous battle, fought in every crisis, every briefing, every moment when her responsibilities threaten to eclipse her identity. She must learn to protect her inner self with the same vigilance she uses to protect her nation's interests. She must set boundaries even when the world resists them. She must learn to rest even when rest feels indulgent. She must allow herself to feel even when feeling seems dangerous.

Her humanity is not a weakness. It is her strength. It enables her to connect, empathise, negotiate sincerely, and represent her country with authenticity. It allows her to see beyond policy to the lives it affects. It brings compassion into spaces that often lack it. Her humanity is not a liability; it is her greatest asset. However, it also makes her more vulnerable.

Therefore, she perseveres with steadiness, quiet determination, and a resolute commitment to safeguarding it. She endeavours to remain whole in a world that fosters fragmentation. She aims to remain gentle in a system that values hardness. She seeks to stay present amid conflicting pressures. She strives to retain her authentic self in a world that continually urges her to assume an alternative identity.

Lesson Learnt

Sofia's experience in Warsaw reveals that emotional containment is not a sign of strength but a cost, paid quietly, consistently, and often invisibly. She learns that the battle to preserve her humanity is not fought in grand gestures but in small, deliberate acts of self-protection.

She discovers that vulnerability is not the opposite of professionalism but its foundation, the source of her empathy, clarity, and authenticity. She realises that compartmentalisation may sustain her temporarily, but only tenderness can restore her. She learns that her humanity is not something to suppress but something to safeguard. And she understands that the strength she is admired for is not the absence of emotion but the courage to carry it with dignity.

Ultimately, Sofia's journey teaches her that emotional containment is not merely a burden; it is a reminder of her depth, resilience, and capacity to remain human in a world that often demands otherwise.

Through this inner battle, she becomes not only a diplomat but a woman who refuses to lose herself, a woman who persists, not unharmed, but unbroken.

CHAPTER SEVENTEEN

The Burden of Being the Exception

The Weight of Firsts

A profound responsibility rests on the shoulders of the female diplomat who becomes the first, the first in her ministry, her mission, her region, her family, or her generation. The world celebrates her appointment, applauds her breakthrough, and frames her achievement as progress. But behind the applause lies a quieter truth: being the first is not only an honour. It is a burden, an obligation, and a test of endurance, identity, and courage. The first woman does not merely enter a room. She walks into history. She walks into expectation. She walks into scrutiny.

Deputy High Commissioner Zara Adelaide understood this intimately upon her arrival in Brussels. She entered a domain where her identity was immediately apparent. She was the youngest participant in the room, the only woman at her level, and the sole African diplomat within a committee that had remained unchanged for decades. Each meeting felt like a performance, every remark scrutinised, every silence interpreted, every achievement magnified. The potential for error felt catastrophic.

Being perceived as an exception meant she could not simply perform her duties; she had to justify her presence.

She had to prove that her appointment was more than symbolic, that she belonged in a space where no woman from her country had previously stood. She had to demonstrate that her leadership was not an anomaly but a precedent.

The Visibility That Exhausts

The challenge of being recognised as an exception begins with visibility. She is seen before she speaks and judged before she acts. She is evaluated not only as an individual but as a representative of all the women who may follow. Her success becomes a benchmark. Her errors become warnings. Her presence becomes a test of whether women deserve to be in such rooms. This visibility is not flattering. It is exhausting.

Zara felt the scrutinising gaze directed at her, curious, cautious, sometimes sceptical. She sensed it in the way her delegation watched her, not for leadership but for perfection. She felt it in her need to prepare twice as thoroughly, speak with twice the precision, and navigate with twice the caution. She understood she could not afford a moment of uncertainty, because it would not be read as human; it would be read as proof that she did not belong.

The Burden of Representation

Being the exception also means bearing the burden of representation. She is not merely herself; she becomes a symbol of progress, possibility, and transformation. She carries an unspoken narrative she did not write, a narrative that demands her success not only for her own sake but for those who will follow. She becomes the bridge between what has been and what could be. But bridges are walked on.

There is also the burden of isolation. Few understand the complexity of her position. She cannot confide easily. Vulnerability is misread as weakness. Failure is amplified. Rest feels impossible. She cannot simply be a diplomat. She must be a pioneer. And pioneers walk alone.

The Emotional Cost of Exceptionality

The emotional burden of being the exception is profound. She absorbs microaggressions in silence. She navigates condescension without confrontation. She maintains composure amid subtle exclusion. She pretends not to notice when her ideas are dismissed until others repeat them. She conceals the sting when her expertise is questioned, unlike her colleagues. She remains steadfast, not because she is unshakable, but because the circumstances demand resilience.

But the burden is not only external. It is internal, the pressure she places on herself, the fear of disappointing those who believe in her, the anxiety of carrying a legacy she did not choose, and the weight of knowing her journey extends beyond her own life. It is the tension between ambition and responsibility, authenticity and self-protection, and expression and survival.

The Quiet Elegance of Breaking Ground

Yet there is an elegance to being the exception. It lies in opening doors once sealed, in expanding an entire generation's imagination, and in proving that leadership is not confined by gender. It lies in the courage to stand where no woman has stood before and to do so with dignity. It lies in understanding that her presence is not merely personal but historical.

Zara felt this elegance one evening after a long day of negotiations. She received a message from a young diplomat in training: "Seeing you in that role makes me believe I can do it too." The sentence was simple, yet it carried the weight of everything she had endured. In that moment, she realised that the burden of being an exception is also a gift, the gift of possibility, representation, influence, and legacy.

The Legacy She Leaves Behind

Being the exception is not easy. It is not glamorous. It is not effortless. It is a journey of courage, resilience, and quiet strength. However, the woman who stands as the exception does not walk alone indefinitely. She walks so that others may follow. She bears the burden so that others may bear less. She breaks new ground so that others may walk it with ease. She becomes the beginning of a narrative that will endure beyond her.

In this realisation, she finds her strength, not in being the first, but in ensuring she will not be the last.

Lessons Learnt

Zara Adelaide's journey reveals that being the first is not merely an achievement; it is a profound emotional and psychological responsibility. The chapter teaches that the woman who becomes the first in her ministry, mission, region, or generation carries a burden that extends far beyond her job description. She must navigate visibility that exhausts, scrutiny that magnifies her every move, and expectations that demand perfection. Her presence becomes symbolic, her performance becomes political, and her mistakes become collective warnings. *In this reality, she learns that being the first is not only an honour but also a test of endurance, identity, and courage.*

The chapter also shows that the burden of representation is both external and internal. Externally, she carries the hopes of those who will follow, the doubts of those who question her, and the biases of those who have never seen someone like her in that space. Internally, she carries the fear of disappointing those who believe in her, the pressure to justify her presence, and the weight of knowing that her journey is larger than her own life. She learns that the emotional cost of exceptionality is real, the microaggressions she absorbs, the isolation she endures, and the quiet resilience she must cultivate to survive rooms not designed for her.

Yet the chapter also reveals the quiet elegance of breaking ground. Zara discovers that being the exception is not only a burden but a legacy. Her presence expands the imagination of those who watch her. Her courage opens doors once sealed. Her resilience becomes a blueprint for others. She realises that the weight she carries is also a gift, the gift of possibility, representation, and transformation. In the message from the young diplomat who sees herself in Zara, she recognises that her journey is not in vain.

Ultimately, she learns that her strength does not lie in being the first, but in ensuring she will not be the last. The woman who stands as the exception becomes the beginning of a narrative that will outlive her. She walks alone so that others may walk with ease. She bears the burden so that others may bear less. And in this realisation, she finds her power not in perfection but in purpose; not in visibility but in legacy.

CHAPTER EIGHTEEN

The Female Diplomat and the Sacred Work of Holding Her Nation's Story

The Story

There is a sacred work the female diplomat performs that few ever name: she becomes the living storyteller of her nation. Not the storyteller of myths or slogans, but the storyteller of truth, the truth of who her people are, what they have survived, what they dream of, and what they refuse to become again. She carries this story in her voice, posture, and presence. She carries it in the way she listens, negotiates, and responds to provocation. She carries it in the way she refuses to let her nation be reduced to stereotypes or statistics.

This sacred work is not ceremonial.

It is lived.

Before she enters any room, she knows she is walking in with centuries behind her, the triumphs, the wounds, the contradictions, the brilliance, the unfinished work. She knows that every sentence she speaks will be interpreted not as the opinion of one woman, but as the reflection of millions. She knows that the world often forms its understanding of her country not from books or lived experience, but from the words she chooses, the tone she uses, and the dignity she embodies.

This is why the female diplomat speaks with intention.

This is why she listens with precision.

This is why she stands with a posture that says, *I know where I come from.*

The Need to Protect Her Nation's Image

During a regional summit in Addis Ababa, Ambassador Farida Suleiman found herself in a tense exchange with a delegation that repeatedly misrepresented her country's history. They spoke of her nation as fragile, unstable, perpetually dependent. They spoke with the confidence of those who had never walked her streets, never met her people, never understood the resilience woven into the fabric of her homeland.

Farida listened, not with anger, but with clarity. She had learned long ago that anger clouds the truth, while clarity reveals it. She watched the way the delegates spoke, the way they leaned back in their chairs, the way they used phrases like "your people" and "your situation," as though her nation were a case study rather than a sovereign state.

When it was her turn to speak, she did not recite policy.

She told a story.

She spoke of the women who rebuilt communities after conflict, women who carried bricks on their heads and hope in their hands. She spoke of the farmers who fed entire regions during drought, refusing to let hunger define their destiny. She spoke of the young innovators who created solutions with limited resources, proving that brilliance is not the privilege of wealthy nations. She spoke of the elders who preserved wisdom across generations, reminding the world that knowledge is not always written in books. She spoke of the dignity her people carried even in hardship.

The room shifted.

Not because she argued, but because she revealed.

She reminded them that nations are not headlines.
They are human beings.
They are memories.
They are courageous.
They are complex.

Her story did not erase the challenges her nation faced.
It contextualised them.
It dignified them.
It reframed them.

Her Narrative

Farida's sacred work did not end in Addis Ababa. It followed her home, into the quiet spaces where diplomacy meets identity. One evening, after returning from a long mission, she visited her mother in the small coastal town where she had grown up. Her mother, a retired schoolteacher, sat on the veranda peeling oranges, the scent of citrus filling the air.

"You looked tired on television," her mother said gently.

Farida smiled. "It was a long day."

Her mother placed an orange segment in Farida's hand. "You carry us well."

It was a simple sentence, yet it carried the weight of generations. Her mother was not speaking of the speech Farida had delivered or the negotiation she had led. She was speaking of the story, the story Farida carried into rooms where her people had never been invited before.

Later that night, Farida walked through her childhood neighbourhood. Children played football in the dusty street. Women sat outside their homes, braiding each other's hair. Men gathered around a radio, listening to the evening news. These were the people she represented, not the diplomats in tailored suits, not the analysts writing reports, not the commentators on television. These were the people whose stories she carried.

She paused at the edge of the street, watching the children laugh.
This is the truth the world never sees, she thought.
This is the story I must protect.

When Her Nation Is Tested

Months later, during a crisis meeting in Geneva, Farida found herself once again defending her nation's narrative. A humanitarian report had been released, painting her country in broad, simplistic strokes as a place of suffering, instability, and perpetual need. The report was not entirely wrong, but it was incomplete. It lacked nuance. It lacked humanity. It lacked the voices of the people who lived the reality it described.

During the meeting, a delegate from a powerful country said, "Your nation must accept that it cannot manage its own affairs."

Farida felt the words land like stones.
But she did not flinch.

She leaned forward, her voice steady. "My nation has managed its affairs through colonisation, through conflict, through drought, through political transition. We have managed our affairs when the world turned its back on us. We have managed our affairs when no one believed we could.

Do not mistake struggle for incapacity. Do not mistake challenge for weakness. Do not mistake resilience for dependence."

The room fell silent.

She continued, "If you want to understand my nation, you must listen to its people, not just its problems."

It was not a speech.
It was a correction.
A restoration.
A reclaiming.

The Story She Tells Herself

There is another layer to the sacred work of the female diplomat, the story she must tell herself. The story that keeps her grounded when the world misnames her people. The story that reminds her of why she stands in rooms where she is underestimated. The story that strengthens her when she is tired, discouraged, or feels the weight of representation pressing on her shoulders.

Farida often repeated a quiet mantra before entering high-stakes meetings: *I am not here to impress. I am here to represent.*

Representation is not performance.
It is presence.
It is a responsibility.
It is truth-telling.

She understood that her voice carried the echoes of women who had never been allowed to speak. She understood that her presence challenged narratives written without her people. She understood that her dignity was a form of diplomacy.

Lessons Learnt

She learns that the sacred work of holding her nation's story is not loud, but it is powerful. She discovers that storytelling is not a soft skill; it is a diplomatic strategy. She realises that the world does not change when she argues; it changes when she reveals. And she understands that her greatest contribution is not the agreements she signs, but the dignity she restores through truth.

She becomes the guardian of her nation's narrative, not by embellishing, not by exaggerating, but by telling the kind of truth that humanises, dignifies, and reframes.

The female diplomat does not carry her nation's story as a burden. She carries it as a calling.

CHAPTER NINETEEN

The City That Holds Its Breath: Navigating Fragile Peace in Prague

A City Suspended Between Calm and Memory

Prague in late autumn radiates a distinctive stillness, a suspended calm that makes the city feel as though it is holding its breath. The air is crisp, carrying the scent of woodsmoke and damp stone. The Vltava River flows with deliberate quiet, mirroring the soft glow of streetlamps that flicker to life before dusk. This is a city that remembers its ruptures. It has learned to read tremors beneath political serenity, to recognise when peace is not permanent but merely resting.

It was into this atmosphere that Minister Councillor Layla Al-Hashimi arrived for her assignment. A seasoned diplomat from Oman, she was known for her clarity of thought and her ability to perceive emotional undercurrents long before they surfaced. Her career had taken her to postings near conflict zones, to tribal mediation tables, and into delicate cultural negotiations. But Prague presented a different challenge, not the volatility of open conflict, but the fragility of a peace that could be disturbed by a single miscalculation.

The Quiet Tension Beneath Official Mandates

Her mandate, as outlined by headquarters, appeared straightforward: strengthen bilateral cooperation to counter rising misinformation campaigns targeting Middle Eastern communities across Central Europe. Yet beneath the formal language lay a more intricate reality, an escalation in xenophobic rhetoric, several troubling incidents involving Arab students, and a political climate that shifted unpredictably with each news cycle.

Layla sensed the tension immediately upon entering the embassy's ornate reception hall. It was not hostility but uncertainty, the kind that makes people speak more softly, move more cautiously, and observe their surroundings with heightened vigilance.

Within days, her schedule filled with meetings: university rectors concerned about student safety, civil society organisations advocating for intercultural dialogue, and Czech officials attempting to maintain stability without publicly acknowledging the rising unease. She listened, observed, and responded with the composed professionalism expected of her. She coordinated with the embassy's Consular and Political Sections, drafted policy memos, liaised with the Ministry of Interior and local police units, and reassured anxious parents in Muscat and beyond.

The Incident That Shifted the Atmosphere

The true test arrived quietly, without ceremony. On a cold evening, as fog settled over the Charles Bridge like a pale veil, the embassy received a report: three Arab students had been harassed on Tram 22. The incident involved verbal slurs, a passenger recording them mockingly, and a brief confrontation that left the students shaken. No physical harm occurred, but within hours, distorted versions of the event spread online, fuelled by speculation, inflammatory commentary, and coordinated misinformation accounts.

The situation escalated rapidly. The embassy activated its rapid alert protocol, notifying the Ambassador, the security officer, and the crisis communication team. Layla was summoned to an emergency meeting at the Ministry of Interior. The room was tense, with competing priorities hanging in the air. Some officials attempted to minimise the incident. Others feared diplomatic fallout. A few suggested the students had "misinterpreted cultural cues."

Layla listened with hands folded neatly, her expression composed. Internally, she felt the familiar constriction, the diplomat's burden of balancing truth with tact, urgency with restraint, protection with diplomacy.

She waited until the room had exhausted its evasions. Then she spoke.

"This is not about blame," she said, her voice steady but carrying quiet authority. "It is about ensuring that every student, Czech or foreign, feels safe in this city. If we treat this lightly, we allow fear to grow where trust should be."

The room fell silent, not in agreement, but in recognition. She had articulated what no one else dared to voice.

The Weight She Carries Alone

After the meeting, she stepped into the cold night. Fog blurred the city's contours. She walked along the river, her breath forming small clouds. The day's weight settled into her shoulders, not the weight of crisis, but the weight of responsibility, which presses inward rather than downward. She paused on the bridge, watching the water move beneath her. In that moment, she allowed herself to feel what she could not express in the meeting: the ache of being the one who must always remain composed, the one who absorbs tension without releasing her own, the one who carries her community's fears while projecting confidence.

Yet Prague offered her something unexpected, a contemplative solitude that did not feel like loneliness. The city's calm mirrored her inner discipline. Its history reminded her that fragility and resilience often coexist. She found sanctuary in small rituals: a morning walk through Old Town Square before tourists arrived, an hour in a café where the barista learned her name, the gentle chime of tram bells echoing through narrow streets. These moments grounded her. They reminded her that diplomacy is not only the art of negotiation but the art of maintaining one's humanity in environments that demand perpetual restraint.

The Slow Work of Restoring Stability

In the weeks that followed, Layla worked closely with Czech partners to establish a rapid response mechanism for incidents involving international students. It included a joint hotline, coordinated police-university protocols, and a communication channel between the embassy's political section and the Ministry of Interior. She organised intercultural dialogue sessions with student associations, community leaders, and civil society groups. She met privately with the affected students, listening with a tenderness she rarely displayed publicly.

Gradually, almost imperceptibly, the atmosphere shifted. Not dramatically, but steadily. The city exhaled.

And in that exhale, Layla recognised the deeper lessons Prague had been teaching her, lessons not written in policy manuals but lived in the quiet spaces between crisis and calm.

The Lessons Prague Whispered

Fragile peace necessitates proactive diplomacy. Threats to stability do not invariably originate from explosions or declarations; they frequently manifest through whispers, rumours, and subtle shifts in public sentiment. A diplomat must identify these early indicators. Information crises tend to progress more rapidly than institutions can respond. The tram incident exemplified how misinformation can surpass official communication, thereby requiring diplomacy that is both agile and precise.

Emotional resilience must be complemented by institutional coordination. Her restraint was significant; however, it was the collaboration among the embassy, universities, and Czech authorities that ultimately upheld stability. Cultural engagement constitutes a form of security.

Dialogue sessions were not merely symbolic gestures; they served as preventive measures.

Building trust diminishes susceptibility to manipulation.

Crisis response must safeguard both individuals and the environment they inhabit. Her responsibilities extended beyond incident management to restoring a sense of safety. Quiet authority can influence institutional behaviour. Her measured intervention altered the meeting's tone without resulting in confrontation. Furthermore, diplomacy is fundamentally rooted in humanity, rather than protocol.

A female diplomat's private rituals were not mere indulgences; they were vital to her capacity for survival.

The City That Finally Exhaled

As she crossed the Charles Bridge one evening, the fog lifting just enough for the castle lights to shimmer through, Layla sensed that the city was no longer holding its breath. It was listening. Layla, Arab diplomat, woman, custodian of delicate truths, walked forward with the composed confidence of someone who understands that peace is not the absence of tension, but the courage to manage it with grace.

CHAPTER TWENTY

Reclaiming the Diplomatic Voice in a Forceful Silence

When Silence Becomes a Form of Harm

There comes a point in a female diplomat's career when silence becomes a strategic tool rather than a form of harm. Initially, silence may serve as a means of observation, enabling her to assess her environment, interpret social cues, and comprehend the underlying power dynamics before actively engaging. It enhances her perceptiveness, refines her intuition, and imparts the understanding of unspoken rules within spaces not inherently designed with her in consideration.

However, over time, a different form of silence begins to manifest around her, one that is not consciously chosen, deliberate, or strategic. This silence arises when her contributions are disregarded, her expertise is redirected, and her presence is acknowledged without substantive engagement. Such silence does not serve as a shield but effectively erases her presence.

For Ambassador Sofia Marković, this distinction was not merely theoretical but manifested as a tangible and persistent reality. It unfolded gradually, persistently, until it became undeniable. She had dedicated years to navigating multilateral corridors, often being the sole woman at the negotiation table, the youngest voice in the room, and the only individual who had traversed the aftermath of conflicts under discussion.

She mastered the art of precise speaking, recognising that errors could be unforgiving.

Sofia learned to listen intently, understanding that silence could function as a form of power. Nonetheless, she also became aware of silences that were not voluntary, imposed by institutions that purported to value inclusion.

This was not simply a matter of personality or style. It was not about being shy or reserved. It was about the way the room responded to her presence. It was about who was allowed to interrupt and who was expected to endure interruption. It was about whose comments were taken as definitive and whose were treated as supplementary. It was about whose lived experience was treated as data and whose was treated as anecdote. Over time, Sofia began to understand that what she was experiencing was not just individual disregard. It was institutional complicity in her erasure.

Silence, in this context, was not neutral.

It was not empty.

It was active.

It was a mechanism through which the institution preserved its familiar hierarchies.

It was a way of maintaining the comfort of those who had always been heard by ensuring that those who had not were kept at the margins. The silence around her was not an absence of sound. It was the presence of a structure that had decided, long before she arrived, whose voice would be treated as central and whose would be treated as optional.

When the Institution Revealed Itself

The moment this reality crystallised for Sofia came at a high-level forum on post-conflict reconstruction in Brussels. She had been invited as the lead expert, a formal recognition of her years spent working with displaced communities in the Balkans. She had walked through villages where bullet holes still marked houses. She had sat with women who could not bury their dead because the bodies had never been found. She had negotiated with men who carried both weapons and grief. Her expertise was not theoretical. It was embodied.

That morning, the room was filled with ministers, ambassadors, senior officials, and young diplomats. The banners spoke of inclusion, resilience, and sustainable peace. The programme's language emphasised participation and diversity. On paper, the institution appeared enlightened. But as the panel began, the deeper architecture of the space revealed itself.

The moderator introduced Sofia with a brief sentence, then spent several minutes elaborating on the achievements of the male panellists. When the first question, a question directly related to community-based reconciliation, was posed, it was directed to a male ambassador who had never worked in the region.

Sofia waited.

She assumed it was an oversight.

The second question, on trauma-informed peacebuilding, was again directed away from her. She watched as the moderator's gaze moved past her, as though her presence were decorative rather than essential.

At first, she tried to rationalise it. Perhaps the moderator was nervous. Perhaps he had been given a list of names and was following it mechanically. But as the pattern persisted, the explanation shifted. This was not nervousness. This was not an accident. This was a performance of institutional habit. The institution, through the moderator, was doing what it had always done: centring certain voices and marginalising others, even when the marginalised voice was the most qualified to speak.

When the moderator attempted to bypass her yet again, directing a question on gender and peacebuilding to a male colleague who had never led a programme in that field, Sofia felt something in her settle. She leaned forward, placed her hand gently on the table, and spoke in a calm but unyielding tone.

"I would like to address that question," she said. "It speaks directly to the work my team and I have led for the past decade."

The room fell silent. It was not the silence of discomfort alone. It was the silence of a structure being interrupted. For a brief moment, the institution's choreography faltered. The moderator hesitated, then nodded. The microphone was passed to her.

Sofia did not raise her voice. She did not perform outrage. She spoke with clarity, precision, and the authority of lived experience. She described the women's committees that had become informal courts of justice in villages where formal systems had collapsed.

She spoke of the quiet negotiations that took place in kitchens and courtyards, far from conference halls.

She spoke of the emotional labour required to rebuild trust in communities where neighbours had turned against one another. She spoke of the cost of asking women to testify about their suffering in public spaces that were not designed to hold their pain.

As she spoke, the atmosphere in the room shifted. Some faces softened. Others tightened. A few looked away. But the structure had been disturbed. The silence that had been used to contain her had been broken, not by volume, but by insistence. When she finished, the applause that followed was not merely for her eloquence.

It was for the truth she had forced the room to confront.

After the session, a young diplomat approached her. “You showed me something I didn’t know how to name,” she said. “You showed me what it looks like to refuse erasure without becoming what they fear.”

Sofia smiled, not out of triumph, but out of recognition. She understood that what had happened in that room was not simply a personal victory. It was a small rupture in a much larger structure.

Silence as Structural Violence

In the days that followed, Sofia found herself returning to the experience, not as a memory, but as a case study. She began to think of silence not only as a personal burden but as a form of structural violence. Structural violence is not always visible. It does not always announce itself with dramatic gestures. It is often quiet, procedural, and polite. It is embedded in who is invited to speak, who is introduced with gravitas, who is given time to elaborate, and who is gently moved along.

In diplomatic culture, structural violence often appears as decorum. It hides behind phrases such as “time constraints,” “protocol,” and “established practice.” It is evident in the way agendas are drafted, the order of speakers, the allocation of speaking time, and the unspoken rules about who may interrupt whom. It is evident in the assumption that certain accents carry more authority, that certain bodies are more naturally associated with expertise, and that certain experiences are more easily translated into policy.

Silence, in this context, is not simply the absence of speech. It is the outcome of a system that has decided whose voice is necessary and whose is optional. When the female diplomat is consistently spoken over, her interventions summarised by others, and her expertise acknowledged but not centred, the institution is not merely inattentive. It is participating in her erasure. It is enacting a form of harm that leaves no visible scars but inflicts deep intellectual and emotional bruises.

Sofia began to recognise that the burden placed on her to "reclaim her voice" was itself a reflection of institutional complicity. The responsibility was framed as hers: she must be more assertive, more confident, more visible. Yet the deeper question was rarely asked: why must she fight to be heard in an institution that claims to value her presence? Why is the labour of reclaiming voice placed on the one being erased, rather than on the system that erases?

To name silence as structural violence is to shift the focus from individual resilience to institutional responsibility. It is not that she is too quiet, too soft, or too hesitant. The problem is that the institution has normalised a pattern in which her voice is treated as supplementary, even when it is central. It is to insist that the work of transformation cannot rest solely on her capacity to resist. It must also rest on the institution's willingness to change.

The Unforgettable Day

Long before Brussels, another night marked Sofia's journey, a night without microphones, panels, or applause. It was the night her silence was broken in private, before it was broken publicly. She had spent the day in a confidential negotiation over a sensitive regional issue. The room was filled with senior diplomats, predominantly older men who had known each other for decades. Her presence was due to her instrumental role in drafting the framework under discussion.

However, throughout the day, her contributions were often redirected, paraphrased, or absorbed into the collective without proper attribution. When she spoke, her points were briefly acknowledged, then rephrased by others and treated as new. When she paused to reflect, the conversation moved on without returning to her.

By the end of the meeting, she felt as though she had been both present and absent. Her body had been in the room. Her work had been on the table. But her voice had not been allowed to exist fully. She walked back to her hotel through streets that glowed with the soft light of late evening. The city was alive with conversation, but inside her, there was only a dense, heavy quiet.

In her room, she removed her jacket, loosened her hair, and sat on the edge of the bed. The silence felt different from the strategic silence she had once chosen. This silence felt like a weight pressing against her chest. It felt like a verdict. It felt like a story about her being written without her consent.

She lowered her head into her hands and, for the first time in years, allowed herself to say aloud what she had been resisting.

"This cannot be my story."

The words were simple, but not small. They refused. They were a line drawn in the interior space of her own life. In that moment, she was not addressing a moderator, a minister, or a room full of diplomats. She was addressing herself. She acknowledged that the cost of enduring imposed silence was too high. It was not only diminishing her professionally. It was eroding her sense of self.

That night did not end with a grand resolution. There was no sudden surge of confidence, no dramatic vow. What changed was subtler and more profound. She began to understand that reclaiming her voice was not about becoming louder or more aggressive. It was about refusing to participate in her own erasure. It was about recognising that every time she swallowed her words to preserve others' comfort, she was reinforcing the very structure that harmed her.

From that night onward, she began to treat her voice not as a personal asset but as a responsibility. She carried within her the stories of communities that had trusted her with their pain. Allowing herself to be silenced was, in a sense, allowing their experiences to be sidelined as well.

Her voice was not hers alone.

t was a vessel.

The Invisible Labour Behind the Voice

While Sofia was navigating these internal and institutional battles, other women in diplomacy were bearing similar burdens in various forms. Consul General Emilia Novak, stationed in Vienna, experienced a comparable tension that manifested not only in conference rooms but also in the subtle intersections of her professional and personal life.

On a winter morning, Emilia received an urgent call from the capital. A crisis meeting was scheduled for eight o'clock. She was expected to brief the minister directly on a rapidly evolving situation. As she gathered her notes, her phone vibrated with a message from her teenage son.

"Mum, I forgot my presentation at home. It's due in the first period. Please."

Two demands, both urgent, both legitimate. One belonged to the state. The other to her child. The institution would never see the second. It would only see whether she appeared composed, prepared, and punctual on the call. Emilia decided in seconds. She called her driver, grabbed the neatly bound presentation from the dining table, and rode through the snow-lined streets to the school. Her son met her at the gate, breathless with relief. "Thank you," he whispered before running inside. She checked the time. It was 7:32 a.m.

By 7:58 a.m., she was seated at her desk in the consulate, documents spread before her, her voice steady as she briefed the minister. No one on the call knew she had just navigated two crises, one domestic, one diplomatic, with the same precision. No one knew that her composure was not the absence of pressure but its mastery. This, too, is part of the structural violence embedded in diplomatic culture. The institution benefits from the emotional and logistical labour of the female diplomat without acknowledging it. It expects her to be fully present in the room while ignoring the invisible work that makes that presence possible.

It praises her professionalism while remaining indifferent to the cost of maintaining it.

The female diplomat's voice, when she finally speaks, carries more than policy. It carries the weight of all the unseen negotiations she conducts before she ever enters the formal negotiation. It carries the tension of being needed in two places at once. It carries the quiet exhaustion of being indispensable and invisible at the same time.

Reclaiming Voice as Ethical Refusal

To reclaim her voice, then, is not merely to speak. It is to refuse a system that normalises her erasure. It is to insist that her presence is not symbolic but substantive. It is to challenge the institution's comfort with its own patterns. It is to say that the cost of maintaining decorum cannot be the continued silencing of those whose experiences are most essential to the conversation.

Reclaiming her voice is also an ethical act. It is not driven solely by ego or the desire for visibility. It is driven by the recognition that, in certain contexts, silence becomes complicity. If she allows her expertise to be consistently overshadowed and her lived experience to be consistently sidelined, she risks reinforcing the very narratives that harm the communities she represents. Her refusal to disappear is, in this sense, a refusal to allow their realities to be edited out of the institutional record.

This reclamation is not loud for its own sake. It is deliberate. It is measured. It is grounded in the understanding that her voice is not an intrusion into the diplomatic space.

It is an expansion of it.

It is the introduction of truths that the institution has long avoided confronting. It is the insistence that peace cannot be negotiated solely by those who have never had to live with the consequences of its absence.

Lessons Learnt

The female diplomat learns that silence, when imposed, is not a neutral state but a form of structural violence. She comes to understand that the burden of reclaiming her voice has been unfairly framed as a personal challenge, when in reality it exposes institutional complicity in her erasure. She recognises that her voice is not merely an expression of individual opinion, but a vessel for the experiences of those whose lives are rarely represented in official documents. She realises that to remain silent in the face of systematic sidelining is to participate, however unwillingly, in the continuation of that system.

She learns that reclaiming her voice is an ethical refusal, a refusal to disappear, a refusal to treat her expertise as optional, a refusal to let the institution remain unchallenged in its habits. She understands that her presence in the room is not a favour granted by the system, but a necessary correction to its history. She discovers that her task is not to become louder for the sake of loudness, but to become clearer, more anchored, more aligned with the truth she carries.

Ultimately, she understands that reclaiming her voice is not only about her. It is about those who will come after her, who will walk into rooms she has already disturbed. It is about shifting the architecture of diplomacy so that future women do not have to fight the same battles in the same way. And in this understanding, she realises that the female diplomat does not raise her voice to be tolerated.

She raises her presence as a challenge to structural silence, and, slowly, the world begins to adjust.

CHAPTER TWENTY-ONE

Loneliness in Leadership

The Architecture of Solitude

Loneliness extends beyond mere absence; it signifies a profound lack of understanding. For a female diplomat, loneliness takes the form of an architectural construct, a structured framework within which she learns to navigate, inhabit, and ultimately excel. This construct develops gradually and silently over the years, arising from the burden of responsibilities that cannot be shared, decisions that resist explanation, and emotions that are difficult to articulate. It encapsulates the solitude inherent in leadership and the isolation associated with representation, embodying the subtle distance between one's authentic self and the persona one must adopt.

From the female diplomat's perspective, leadership is not merely a role; it is a geographical space, with loneliness serving as its capital city.

Ambassador Laila Mensim encountered this geographical landscape upon her arrival in Addis Ababa to assume her diplomatic duties at the African Union. She entered an environment of considerable historical significance, where each corridor represented legacy, each meeting carried political weight, and every discourse had implications extending well beyond its immediate context. She was prepared for diplomacy, negotiations, and scrutiny.

What she was unprepared for was the solitude intrinsic to being a central figure observed by all, yet genuinely perceived by few.

Responsibility as Isolation

Loneliness in leadership begins with responsibility.

She is the one who must decide when others hesitate.
She is the one who must speak when others remain silent.
She is the one who must hold the centre when others fracture.
She is the one who must absorb the consequences of decisions made in imperfect conditions.

Responsibility isolates her, not because she is alone, but because she cannot share her burdens. There is also a solitude of perception. Others see her title before they see her humanity. They acknowledge her competence yet overlook her exhaustion. They admire her composure yet miss her doubts. They praise her strength yet ignore the toll it exacts. She becomes a symbol, and symbols are admired, not understood.

The Moment the Personal and Political Collide

She experienced this truth with profound clarity during her first major negotiation. The room was filled with seasoned diplomats, each representing national interests that clashed in ways that seemed immovable. She mediated, reframed, redirected, and kept the discussion on track with the precision of someone twice her age. When the meeting concluded, her colleagues congratulated her.

They praised her clarity.
They praised her calm.
They praised her authority.

But no one asked how she felt.

No one asked what it cost her.

No one asked what she needed.

Leadership had elevated her and separated her.

What no one knew was that her phone had vibrated twice during the negotiation. Messages from Daniel, the man she had once imagined a future with. He had written, *"We need to talk," followed by, "I don't know how to reach you anymore."*

She saw the messages only after the meeting ended.

She stared at them for a long moment, feeling the familiar ache of a relationship dissolving, not through conflict, but through distance.

Diplomacy had not taken her love away; it had simply taken her time.

And time had taken everything else.

The Solitude of Emotional Containment

The architecture of solitude also encompasses emotional detachment. She cannot respond impulsively. She cannot reveal uncertainty. She cannot articulate frustration. She cannot display vulnerability in environments where it is misinterpreted as weakness. She must maintain composure even when shaken, remain poised even when overwhelmed, and exhibit diplomacy even when in pain.

Her emotions become private possessions, guarded, confined, and concealed.

There is also the solitude of identity. She is often the only woman in the room. The only African. The only young leader. The only one carrying multiple layers of representation. Her navigation extends beyond diplomacy; she must also navigate perceptions, biases, expectations, and history. This layered identity creates a multifaceted loneliness that is difficult to articulate, even to those who care for her.

The Evening She Finally Allowed Herself to Feel

Laila confronted this truth one evening after an exceptionally intense negotiation. She returned to her residence, removed her shoes, and sat on the floor, choosing it over the couch or desk because it felt more honest and grounding. She closed her eyes and allowed herself to feel the loneliness she had been carrying, not to succumb to it, but to acknowledge, name, and understand it.

Her phone lay beside her, its screen dimmed, Daniel's messages still unread. She knew she should respond, but she also knew she no longer had the emotional space to salvage what was left. Leadership had not only separated her from others; it had quietly separated her from herself. In that moment, she gained a profound insight: loneliness is not the enemy. Unacknowledged loneliness is.

Transforming Loneliness into Clarity

The structure of loneliness becomes manageable, even purposeful, when she learns to inhabit it with awareness rather than fear. It means building windows rather than walls, letting light in and trusting people in. She recognises that effective leadership does not require emotional exile. She adopts small rituals to anchor herself: morning stillness, evening reflection, quiet walks, deliberate pauses. She cultivates relationships that nourish rather than deplete her. She communicates candidly with those she trusts. She learns to rest without guilt and to embrace her humanity without apology.

Gradually, the architecture of loneliness transforms into something else: a sanctuary, a space of clarity, where she reconnects with her purpose.

Leadership will always involve solitude. But solitude need not become suffering.

The Strength the World Will See

The external world may never observe the architecture of loneliness within her. They may never know the cost of her composure, the weight of her silence, or the depth of her private battles. However, they will recognise the strength it fosters. They will acknowledge a diplomat who leads not from seclusion, but from profound understanding; a woman who has mastered inhabiting her solitude with grace, clarity, and unwavering purpose.

Lessons Learnt

Ambassador Laila Mensim's journey reveals that loneliness in leadership is not a flaw, a weakness, or a sign of inadequacy, but an inherent architecture within which the female diplomat must learn to live and lead. The chapter teaches that solitude is woven into the fabric of responsibility, not because she is unsupported, but because the weight she carries cannot be shared, explained, or fully understood by those who look to her for guidance. Leadership elevates her, but it also separates her, creating a quiet distance between her inner world and the public persona she must uphold.

Laila learns that the solitude of leadership is layered. There is the solitude of responsibility, where she must decide when others hesitate. There is the solitude of perception, where she is admired yet unseen. There is the solitude of emotional containment, where she must guard her vulnerabilities to protect her authority. And there is the solitude of identity, where she navigates multiple layers of representation, as a woman, an African, and a young leader, often standing alone in rooms where she carries more history than anyone realises.

Yet the chapter also reveals that loneliness, when acknowledged rather than feared, becomes a source of clarity. Laila discovers that solitude can become a sanctuary when she learns to inhabit it with awareness. Through small rituals, honest reflection, and intentional grounding, she comes to understand that leadership does not require emotional exile. Instead, it requires the courage to recognise her humanity even while carrying others' expectations.

Ultimately, she learns that loneliness does not diminish her; it refines her. It sharpens her intuition, deepens her wisdom, and strengthens her resolve. The woman who can sit with her solitude without losing herself becomes the woman who can lead others without losing them.

In that quiet strength, she discovers that the architecture of loneliness is not a prison but a place where purpose becomes clear, and leadership becomes authentic.

CHAPTER TWENTY-TWO

The Unseen Toll of Cultural Translation

When the Body Speaks Before the Voice

Long before the female diplomat admits she is tired, her body has already spoken. Long before she acknowledges the emotional weight she carries, her body has already begun to bend under it. Long before she whispers the truth of her exhaustion, her body has already been telling the story in ways she has learned to ignore. The body speaks first, quietly, subtly, insistently, long before her voice finds the courage to follow. She feels it in the tension that settles in her shoulders after days of maintaining her posture in rooms where she cannot afford to seem uncertain.

She feels it in the tightness of her jaw after hours of diplomatic restraint, where every word must be measured and every reaction controlled. She feels it in the heaviness in her chest when she carries the emotional residue of crises that do not belong to her but cling to her anyway. She feels it in the fatigue that lingers even after sleep, the kind of tiredness that rest alone cannot cure.

Her body speaks in whispers at first.
Then in murmurs.
Then, in warnings.

But she has been trained to override those signals. She has been taught to prioritise duty over discomfort, responsibility over rest, and composure over vulnerability. She has learned to silence her body as she has learned to silence her emotions, not out of neglect but out of necessity.

The diplomatic world rewards endurance, not embodiment. It rewards steadiness, not softness. It rewards the mind, not the body.

Yet the body keeps speaking.

The Slow Unravelling Beneath Competence

When Political Attaché Zara El Sayed was assigned to Nairobi, she approached her duties with diligence and precision. She attended every meeting, responded promptly to all correspondence, and volunteered for every task. Her clarity, efficiency, and reliability made her indispensable.

But beneath her accomplished exterior, her well-being was beginning to deteriorate.

Her health issues began with frequent, minor headaches she dismissed as dehydration. Then came insomnia, with nights spent staring at the ceiling as her mind replayed conversations and anticipated crises. Soon, chest tightness accompanied tense negotiations, followed by shallow breathing, which she masked with a composed smile. Fatigue eventually took hold, making even simple tasks feel burdensome. She reassured herself that she was fine, that a weekend of rest would fix everything, and that she could push through.

But the body does not negotiate.
It insists.

The Moment Her Body Refused to Stay Silent

During a high-pressure meeting on regional security, Zara experienced a sudden wave of dizziness. The room blurred. Voices faded into a distant hum.

She steadied herself, inhaled quietly, and continued speaking as if nothing had happened. No one noticed. No one asked. No one suspected that her body had issued a warning she could no longer ignore.

What no one knew was that earlier that morning, she had received a voice note from her younger brother back home.

His voice was soft, concerned.

“We miss you. You sound tired. Are you okay?”

She had listened to it in the car, paused it halfway, and told herself she would respond later. She never did. The day swallowed her whole. By evening, the guilt pressed heavier on her chest than the fatigue. She realised she had become fluent in the language of other nations, yet increasingly estranged from the people who loved her most.

That night, alone in her apartment, she sat on the floor with her back against the wall, her breathing shallow, her hands trembling. It was the first time she allowed herself to acknowledge what her body had been trying to communicate for months:

She was not well.
She was exhausted.
She was overwhelmed.
She was carrying more than her body could bear.

The Body as Truth-Teller

The body communicates before the voice, as it lacks diplomacy. It does not negotiate, perform, or pretend. Instead, it conveys the truth even when the mind is unwilling to accept it. It exposes the costs of emotional labour, the toll of perpetual vigilance, and the strain of consistently occupying the role of the steady presence in every setting. It also reveals the truths she conceals from others and from herself.

The female diplomat often learns, sometimes painfully, that neglecting her body is not an act of strength but of self-neglect. Her body is not an impediment to her professional duties; rather, it is the vessel that sustains her through them. It is the instrument through which she listens, negotiates, communicates, and endures. When her body falters, her clarity diminishes. When her body fails, her entire world destabilizes.

Learning to Listen Again

She must cultivate the habit of attentive listening. Attuning to her body is not indulgence; it is intelligence, strategy, and survival. Her clarity depends on rest. Her composure depends on breath. Her resilience depends on nourishment. Her presence depends on grounding.

Listening to her body requires courage, the courage to pause, rest, decline, set boundaries, and acknowledge limits. It requires the bravery to disappoint others to remain true to herself. It requires accepting that she is human, not invincible.

The body communicates in a multitude of languages. Occasionally, this occurs through fatigue, tension, or illness. At times, it manifests through silence, the silence of a body that has reached its limit. Conversely, it also expresses itself through joy, ease, and breath; through the sensation of being entirely present within one's own skin. Her body is not her adversary but her ally; it serves as the compass that guides her back to her true self when external circumstances threaten to distance her from her core.

The Return to Herself

When Zara finally allowed herself to rest, truly rest, she discovered something unexpected.

Her clarity returned.
Her patience deepened.
Her intuition sharpened.
Her presence strengthened.

She became a better diplomat not by pushing harder, but by listening more closely to her body, to her breath, and to the quiet truth she had ignored for too long. The body communicates before the voice because it holds knowledge the mind tries to forget: She cannot serve the world if she abandons herself.

And so, she learns to listen, attentively, persistently, bravely, until her voice and her body finally speak the same truth.

Lessons Learnt

The journey of Zara El Sayed uncovers a profound reality seldom acknowledged in the diplomatic sphere: the body often signals distress long before the voice considers admitting exhaustion. This chapter illustrates that the female diplomat's body serves as the primary testament to her emotional labour, the initial casualty of her perseverance, and the foremost messenger of truths she has been conditioned to conceal. Her headaches, insomnia, chest tightness, and fatigue are not merely inconveniences but are signals, subtle warnings indicating that she has borne more than her humanity can endure.

Zara recognises that neglecting her physical well-being is not a mark of strength but an act of self-neglect. The diplomatic milieu values composure, accuracy, and resilience; yet her body reminds her that she is not a machine but a woman whose well-being directly shapes the clarity of her judgment and the steadiness of her demeanour. This chapter shows that the body is not her adversary; rather, it serves as her compass, guiding her back to her authentic self when the exigencies of diplomacy threaten to detach her from her core.

She discovers that listening to her body is not indulgence but a strategy. Rest becomes a form of intelligence. Boundaries become a form of courage. Stillness becomes a form of survival. When she finally allows herself to pause, her clarity sharpens, her intuition deepens, and her capacity to lead expands. She becomes a better diplomat not by pushing harder, but by honouring the vessel that carries her through every negotiation, crisis, and transition.

Ultimately, the lesson of this chapter is simple yet profound: She cannot serve the world if she abandons herself. Her body is the truth-teller she must learn to trust, the quiet voice that leads her back to balance, presence, and wholeness. When her body and her voice finally speak the same truth, she returns to herself with renewed strength, grounded wisdom, and a deeper understanding of what it means to lead without losing her humanity.

CHAPTER TWENTY-THREE

The Hidden Solitude of Leadership

The Solitude Beneath the Applause

Leadership, especially for female diplomats, is often defined by influence, visibility, and authority. Internationally, it is associated with articulate speech, a self-assured demeanour, and composure in high-level engagements. It encompasses photographs, handshakes, and carefully prepared statements. It celebrates accomplishments, breakthroughs, and moments of success.

But beneath the surface lies a quieter truth, the solitude that accompanies responsibility, the loneliness that intensifies in environments where she must stand alone.

Leadership isolates her not because she is unapproachable, but because she is responsible. It isolates her not because she lacks support, but because she bears the ultimate burden for decisions others merely suggest. It isolates her not because she is emotionally distant, but because she must shield others from the full extent of what she knows. Leadership demands a solitude that is rarely acknowledged, seldom understood, and almost never discussed.

The Weight of Being the Centre

When Ambassador Clara Mendez assumed her posting in Vienna, she stepped into a role many aspired to. She led a mission of significant international prominence, represented her nation at multilateral forums, and oversaw a team of distinguished diplomats.

She commanded respect and admiration and was frequently praised for her clarity and composure. Yet beneath the admiration lay an unforeseen reality: the profound loneliness of being the central figure on whom everyone relied, yet with whom few could truly connect. Her days were filled with meetings, briefings, consultations, and decisions. She listened to her team, guided them, protected them, and advocated for them. She absorbed their concerns, frustrations, and hopes. She carried their burdens alongside her own.

Yet when the door closed behind her at the end of each day, she stepped into a silence heavier than the noise she had left behind. Leadership had placed her at the heart of everything, yet paradoxically at the periphery of everyone.

The Solitude of Expectation

Leadership isolates her through expectation. She is presumed to have answers even when the path is unclear. She must provide solutions amid ambiguity, project confidence despite internal uncertainty, and maintain composure when others unravel. She is the stabilising force, the voice of reason, the anchor in the storm.

But who anchors her?

The female diplomat learns early that leadership does not afford the luxury of vulnerability. She cannot break down in front of her team. She cannot express doubt to her counterparts. She cannot reveal fear to her superiors. She must carry her uncertainties privately and bear her emotional fatigue in silence.

Leadership demands that she embody both humanity and superhuman resilience, a paradox that deepens her solitude.

The Solitude of Secrets

There is also the solitude of confidentiality. She bears knowledge she cannot disclose, even to those she holds dear. She manages sensitive information, classified briefings, delicate negotiations, and political realities that must remain unspoken. She holds truths that shape her decisions, truths that estrange her from others who do not share similar responsibilities.

Confidentiality is a barrier, necessary yet isolating.

Clara experienced this most profoundly in her personal life. Before her time in Vienna, she had maintained a quiet, steady relationship with a man who understood her rhythm. However, as the months passed, their conversations grew increasingly brief, and their calls less frequent.

He would send messages such *as "I miss you" or "When can we talk?"* and she would respond hours later with apologies she intended but could not help but repeat.

Eventually, the messages stopped.

Not out of anger, but resignation.

He had grown tired of loving a woman the world needed more than he did.

Clara never blamed him.

She simply added the loss to the list of things she carried alone.

The Crisis That Revealed Her Solitude

Her solitude became most evident during a crisis in her second year in Vienna. A sudden escalation of a regional conflict turned her mission into a central coordination hub. She worked tirelessly, navigating political sensitivities, managing communications, and making decisions with long-term consequences. Her team praised her strength, clarity, and leadership. But they did not see the nights she spent alone in her office, questioning whether she had made the right call. They did not see the fears she swallowed, the doubts she suppressed, or the weight she carried in silence.

Leadership had made her indispensable and profoundly alone.

The Emotional Distance Leadership Requires

Leadership also requires emotional distance. She must maintain professional boundaries, even with those she cares about. She must balance empathy with authority, warmth with boundaries, and connection with caution. She must be approachable but not vulnerable, supportive but not reliant, present but not exposed. This emotional equilibrium creates a quiet detachment, one that deepens with every promotion, every responsibility, every crisis.

Yet this solitude is not a sign of weakness.

It is evidence of the gravity of her duties, the integrity of her leadership, and the depth of her commitment.

The truth of leadership is simple: the higher she rises, the fewer people she can lean on.

The Ritual That Kept Her Human

Loneliness does not equate to emptiness.

The female diplomat learns to establish her own anchors, rituals, and ways to maintain her humanity. She finds solace in modest acts, such as a cup of tea at dawn, a tranquil walk, and a moment of stillness before the commencement of the day. She derives strength from those who perceive her beyond her professional title, family, and old acquaintances, including mentors who recognise the woman behind the diplomat.

Clara identified her personal anchor in a simple ritual. Each evening, irrespective of how late she returned home, she would light a single candle on her dining table. This seemingly trivial act provided grounding. The flame served as a reminder that she remained human, present, and alive beneath the layers of responsibility. It reaffirmed that leadership did not negate her need for warmth, softness, and quiet truth.

The Strength Found in Solitude

The solitude of leadership teaches her a profound lesson: she must learn to be her own confidante. She must trust her judgement, comfort herself in doubt, and steady herself when the world feels unpredictable. She must master the dual roles of leader and caretaker, diplomat and woman, strength and gentleness. And in that solitude, she uncovers a deeper strength, not the strength gained from others, but the strength that arises from standing firmly within herself.

Leadership will always carry loneliness.
But loneliness does not diminish her.

It refines her.
It deepens her.
It sharpens her intuition, strengthens her resolve, and expands her capacity to lead with wisdom and compassion.

Because the woman who can stand alone without losing herself is the woman who can lead others without losing them.

Lessons Learnt

The story of Ambassador Clara Mendez reveals that leadership is not defined solely by visibility, authority, or public admiration, but by the quiet solitude that accompanies responsibility. She learns that the higher a woman rises in diplomacy, the more she must rely on her inner strength, because leadership often places her at the centre of everything while leaving her with fewer people she can truly lean on. The chapter teaches that solitude is not a punishment but a natural consequence of carrying burdens others do not see and of making decisions others do not have the courage to make.

Clara discovers that leadership demands emotional discipline. She must protect her team from her fears, shield her loved ones from her professional realities, and carry confidential truths that create distance even from those she cares about. She learns that vulnerability is a luxury she cannot always afford, and that the emotional distance required of her is not coldness but responsibility. Her solitude becomes the space where she processes doubt, fear, and uncertainty, not because she is weak, but because she must remain strong for others.

Yet the chapter also reveals that solitude can be a source of profound strength. Through her evening ritual of lighting a single candle, Clara learns to anchor herself, reconnect with her humanity, and remember that leadership does not erase her need for warmth, softness, and stillness. She realises that the ability to stand alone without losing herself refines her intuition, sharpens her judgement, and deepens her compassion.

Ultimately, she learns that leadership always carries loneliness, but that loneliness does not diminish her. It shapes her into a leader who can guide others with wisdom, steadiness, and grace. The woman who can hold herself upright in solitude becomes the woman who can hold others together in moments of crisis. *In that quiet strength, she discovers the true essence of leadership.*

CHAPTER TWENTY-FOUR

Burden and Beauty of Dual Allegiance

The Diplomacy No One Sees

There is a form of diplomacy that unfolds exclusively in the quiet corners of a female diplomat's private life. It is the diplomacy of maintaining her family's unity while upholding her professional responsibilities. It involves the delicate art of balancing official obligations with personal commitments, managing national expectations alongside intimate duties, and fulfilling her official roles while safeguarding the emotional well-being of her loved ones. This form of diplomacy requires no applause, policy documents, or public recognition; however, it demands more of her than any treaty she will ever negotiate.

The international community observes her representing her country with elegance. It does not perceive her absence from birthdays, anniversaries, school performances, and family milestones. It witnesses her speaking confidently at global forums. It does not see her whispering apologies to her children on video calls. It observes her managing crises with composure. It does not see her grappling with guilt in the quiet hours of the night.

The world recognises her strength but remains unaware of the sacrifices that have shaped it.

The Woman Who Carries Two Worlds

When Deputy Head of Mission Elena Duarte was posted to Pretoria, she carried not only her diplomatic portfolio but the fragile ecosystem of her family's life. Her husband took a leave of absence to join her. Her teenage son was adjusting to a new school, a new culture, and a new continent. Her elderly mother remained at home, her health slowly declining. Elena was responsible for all of it, not because she wanted to be, but because the world had quietly entrusted her with that responsibility.

Her days were filled with meetings, negotiations, and representational duties. Her evenings were spent helping with homework, sharing family dinners, and making late-night calls to check on her mother. She moved between worlds with the ease of someone who had learned to separate without breaking. She was the diplomat managing bilateral relations with precision, and the mother managing emotional transitions with tenderness. She was the leader guiding her team through crises, and the wife reassuring her partner that they were still in this together. She was the daughter carrying the weight of distance, and the woman carrying the weight of expectation.

The Negotiations No One Acknowledges

The obligation to maintain her family unit is not an accessory to her diplomatic life; it is woven into every part of it. She negotiates with time, stretching it beyond its limits. She negotiates with guilt, soothing it with the belief that she is doing her best. She negotiates across continents, stitching her family together with love that travels farther than she does. And she negotiates with herself, balancing ambition with compassion, purpose with presence, and duty with desire.

There is a solitude to this form of diplomacy. She must be the emotional anchor for everyone, even when she has no anchor of her own.

She must be strong for her children, steady for her partner, dependable for her parents, and available for her siblings. She is the one who remembers birthdays, sends messages, checks in, and keeps the family narrative alive even when she is thousands of miles away. She must reassure everyone that the distance is temporary, the sacrifices worthwhile, and the bonds unbroken.

The Moment That Broke Her Quietly

But what no one saw was the moment she opened her son's school portal one evening and realised she had missed his first debate competition. He had won second place. He had sent her a picture earlier that day, smiling and holding his certificate, but she had been in a bilateral meeting and only saw it hours later.

She stared at the photo for a long time, pride and grief rising in equal measure.

She whispered, "I'm proud of you," into a room where no one could hear.

It was the kind of moment that quietly breaks a mother.
The kind of moment she carries into every negotiation afterwards.

The Emotional Labour No One Names

The female diplomat learns early that her family's stability often depends on her emotional labour. She becomes the mediator of conflicts, the guardian of traditions, the organiser of holidays, and the bridge between continents. She absorbs the turbulence of relocation, supports her children's adaptation, honours her partner's sacrifices, and manages the grief of missing home.

She becomes the discreet diplomat within her own household, negotiating love, time, and presence with the same skill she brings to international affairs. Yet this diplomacy is not a burden she resents. It is a responsibility she bears with tenderness. Her family grounds her, offers sanctuary, and reminds her of who she is beyond her title. Her work is not separate from her family's story; it is intertwined with it. Her children grow in resilience, adaptability, and global awareness. Her partner's support becomes a quiet pillar of strength. Her parents' pride travels with her into every room she enters.

The Cost and the Beauty

Nonetheless, the cost remains tangible. There are evenings when she quietly weeps after a video call, yearning to be in two places simultaneously. There are mornings when she awakens with an insatiable longing for home that diplomacy alone cannot alleviate.

There are times when she contemplates whether the world comprehends the demands imposed upon her, not merely as a diplomat, but as a woman whose heart spans continents.

However, there are also moments of profound beauty, moments when her child declares, "I'm proud of you."

Moments when her partner gently whispers, "We're in this together."

Moments when her parents assert, "You make us proud."

Moments when her family assembles around her, even though on a screen, and she senses their love sustaining her resilience.

The Woman Who Holds Two Worlds Together

The diplomacy of holding her family together is imperfect. It is not seamless. It is not effortless. It is a living negotiation, a constant recalibration, a delicate balance that requires grace, patience, and forgiveness, especially forgiveness of herself.

But it is also a testament to her capacity to love expansively, to lead compassionately, and to serve without losing the thread of her own humanity.

The woman who can keep her family united while holding the world together is not merely a diplomat.
She is a force.
A bridge.
A quiet architect of both global and personal peace.

And in that duality, that beautiful, impossible duality, she finds the truth of her strength.

Lessons Learnt

The story of Elena Duarte reveals that the most demanding diplomacy is not conducted in embassies or negotiation rooms, but in the intimate spaces of a woman's private life. She learns that dual allegiance to her nation and her family is not a flaw in her design but a defining strength. The story teaches that while the world applauds her public achievements, it remains unaware of the sacrifices that shape her resilience: missed milestones, whispered apologies, and the quiet grief carried between meetings.

Yet these sacrifices do not diminish her; they deepen her humanity. Elena discovers that emotional labour is a form of leadership. The tenderness with which she holds her family together is as significant as the composure she brings to international affairs. Her ability to negotiate across continents while nurturing the emotional stability of her loved ones testifies to her capacity to love expansively and lead compassionately.

She learns that guilt and longing are companions of her calling, not evidence of inadequacy. That forgiveness, especially of herself, is essential to sustaining both her purpose and her peace.

Ultimately, she realises that her dual role is not a burden but a quiet form of power. The same woman who steadies her family through distance is the one who steadies nations through uncertainty. Her life becomes proof that diplomacy is not only the art of managing global relations but also the art of preserving the bonds that anchor her identity.

In holding two worlds together, *she discovers the truth of her strength: she is a bridge, a force, and a quiet architect of both global and personal peace.*

CHAPTER TWENTY-FIVE

The Unspoken Rules

The Untaught Laws

There are unwritten rules in diplomacy that are neither documented nor included in training manuals or policy papers. They are not taught in academic programmes or formal briefings. They form the invisible scaffolding of the diplomatic world, the unspoken laws that female diplomats must master to survive, succeed, and preserve their integrity. They shape her interactions, presence, decisions, silences, and voice. They govern the space between formal protocol and lived reality, determining how she is perceived long before she speaks.

The unspoken rules extend beyond protocol.
They are about power.
They are about perception.
They are about survival.

The First Rule: Presence Must Be Cultivated

When First Secretary Laila Ben Amin arrived in Brussels, she quickly realised that the written rules were the easiest part of her job. She could memorise procedures, study policy frameworks, and master negotiation techniques. But the real diplomacy, the diplomacy that determined influence, access, and credibility, lived in the shadows of the written world.

It lived in the pauses, the glances, the tones, the seating arrangements, the timing of interventions, and the subtle hierarchies that no one acknowledged but everyone obeyed.

The first unspoken rule she learned was this: competence is presumed, but presence must be cultivated. Brilliance alone was insufficient. She needed to be visible without being forceful, confident without being intimidating, and assertive without inviting dismissal. She needed to speak at the right moment, neither too early nor too late, and in the right tone. She learned to read the room before entering, to gauge the emotional temperature before contributing, and to adjust her presence before speaking.

Diplomacy, she realised, was not only about words; it was about how she inhabited space.

The Second Rule: Relationships Shape Outcomes

The second unspoken rule was more subtle: relationships matter more than arguments. Decisions were often shaped in corridors rather than in conference rooms. Alliances were built over coffee rather than in formal statements. Trust was earned through consistency rather than eloquence.

She discovered that the most consequential conversations happened after meetings, when formalities dissolved and truth emerged.

She learned that diplomacy was not only about policy; it was fundamentally about people.

The Third Rule: She Will Be Judged Differently

The third unspoken rule was the most painful: she would be judged differently.
Not always openly.
Not always consciously.
But consistently.

Her mistakes would be remembered longer.
Her successes would be scrutinised more intensely.
Her authority would be tested more frequently.

She would need to be twice as prepared, twice as precise, and twice as composed. She would need to navigate unspoken biases, unacknowledged assumptions, and inherently unfair expectations. Her presence disrupted established patterns, and disruption always carried a cost. She learned this truth one afternoon at a routine coordination meeting. She offered a measured, strategic suggestion, aligned with the discussion. The room fell silent. Moments later, a senior colleague repeated her idea almost word-for-word. This time, the room nodded in agreement.

No one acknowledged that the idea had been hers.
No one looked in her direction.

She sat still, her face composed, her breathing steady, mastering the unspoken rule she had just learned: brilliance is not always enough when spoken from the wrong mouth.

It was a quiet humiliation, the kind that does not wound the ego but bruises the spirit. She carried that bruise into every room after, not as bitterness but as awareness.

The Fourth Rule: Silence Is a Tool

The fourth unspoken rule gradually revealed itself: silence is not emptiness; it is strategy. Silence can disarm, unsettle, and create space for truth. It can shield, protect, or empower her. Speaking less did not mean knowing less; it meant choosing her moment.

She learned that silence could reveal more than words ever could.

The Fifth Rule: Identity Must Be Guarded

The fifth unspoken rule shaped her most profoundly: she must never forget who she is, even when the environment tries to reshape her. Diplomatic spaces are designed to influence, refine, and contain identity. She learned to protect her core values, intuition, and sense of self. Authenticity was not a liability; it was her compass.

She realised she could adapt without disappearing, grow without erasing herself, and belong without surrendering her individuality.

The Personal Moment That Clarified Everything

One evening, after a long day of negotiations, she returned to her apartment to find a message from her younger sister back home. It was a short video of their family gathered for a celebration she had forgotten was taking place that day.

Her sister's voice said, "We miss you. It's not the same without you."

Laila watched the video twice.

Then a third time.

Then she sat on the edge of her bed, the weight of the day settling into her bones. She realised that mastering the unspoken rules came at a cost, not only to her spirit but also to the parts of her life that existed outside the diplomatic world. She was learning to navigate a system that demanded constant vigilance, yet she was also learning to hold on to the pieces of herself that the system could not be allowed to take.

The Mastery That Becomes Her Armour

Laila mastered the unspoken rules not through instruction but through experience, missteps, observation, and the silent wisdom gained from being underestimated and then surpassing expectations. She learned to interpret the unspoken with the same precision she applied to official documents. She learned to navigate with grace, intellect, and the quiet confidence of someone who understood that true power is rarely declared; it is demonstrated.

The unspoken rules became her armour.
They became her strategy.
They became her silent advantage.

But they also became her burden.

Mastering them required vigilance, emotional labour, and constant awareness. She had to anticipate reactions, manage perceptions, and adapt to shifting expectations.

She bore the weight of representation, scrutiny, and exceptionality.

The Woman Who Rises Anyway

She did not falter. She adapted. She evolved. She rose. Because the female diplomat comprehends an essential truth: The unspoken rules may influence the world she enters, but they do not determine the woman she becomes.

She learns these rules.

She masters them.

She employs them.

Yet, she is never subjugated by them. In this silent, deliberate, and powerful mastery, she delineates her own space in a world that previously presumed she did not belong.

Lessons Learnt

Laila Ben Amin's journey reveals that the most powerful forces in diplomacy are not written in manuals or taught in classrooms. The chapter teaches that the female diplomat must master an entire world of unspoken rules, subtle, invisible, and deeply consequential, to survive, be heard, and lead with integrity. She learns that competence alone is never enough; presence must be cultivated, relationships nurtured, and perception managed with precision. Her influence is shaped not only by what she says, but by how she enters a room, how she reads its temperature, and how she positions her voice within its unspoken hierarchies.

The chapter also shows that the unspoken rules carry an emotional cost. Laila discovers that she will be judged differently, scrutinised more intensely, and tested more frequently than her peers.

She learns that brilliance can be dismissed when spoken by the wrong mouth, and that silence can be a strategic tool rather than a void. She realises that diplomacy demands constant vigilance, the ability to anticipate reactions, navigate biases, and adapt without losing herself. Mastering these rules becomes both her armour and her burden, a quiet discipline that requires emotional labour, resilience, and self-awareness.

Ultimately, she learns that the most important unspoken rule is the one she must guard within herself: the rule of identity. She discovers that she can adapt without disappearing, belong without surrendering her individuality, and rise without allowing the system to reshape her core. The unspoken rules may influence the world she enters, but they do not define the woman she becomes. In mastering them, she gains not only a strategic advantage but also inner clarity. She rises not because the rules favour her, but because she understands them and refuses to be diminished by them.

PART III

THE EVOLUTION OF IDENTITY AND LEADERSHIP

"She negotiates with the strength of someone who has already counted the cost."- Kemi.

ARCHITECTURAL PRELUDE

There comes a point in every diplomatic endeavour when external observations can no longer fully explain the internal changes occurring within the woman who drives these processes. Titles, postings, achievements, and crises managed do not capture the subtle revolutions unfolding beneath the surface. Part III describes the realm in which these revolutions unfold.

This stage marks the point at which identity begins to unravel, not through disintegration but through recalibration. The diplomat who reaches this point is no longer the woman of Part I, nor the one who endured the emotional and institutional sacrifices detailed in Part II. She stands at a pivotal juncture between her previous self and the persona she is evolving into. Part III is not about legacy. It is about transition.

It is not about mastery.

It is about metamorphosis.

It is not about the authority she will one day embody. It is about the interior architecture that must be rebuilt before that authority can emerge. Here, leadership is stripped of performance. Identity is stripped of expectation. What remains is the raw material of the self, the parts she has hidden, the parts she has lost, and the parts she must now reclaim. This is where she confronts the quiet truths she has carried across borders, the emotional cartography etched into her by years of service, and the subtle ways diplomacy has shaped, stretched, and sometimes fractured her sense of self.

Part III explores the cycles of identity that diplomacy forces her to navigate, the soft power she learns to wield not as a strategy but as a presence, the losses she absorbs, of time, belonging, certainty, and sometimes herself, the reconstruction that follows every unravelling, and the hidden self that emerges when the performance of diplomacy is no longer enough.

This is the part of the book where she begins to understand that leadership is not only what she offers the world but what she must first offer herself: coherence, clarity, and the courage to evolve.

Part III is the hinge between endurance and emergence. Between the woman shaped by the institution and the woman shaped by her own becoming. Between the identity she inherited and the one she is now intentionally constructing.

This is not the arrival.

This is the becoming.

This is the quiet, interior evolution that prepares her for the sovereignty, conviction, and authorship that will define Part IV.

This is the woman the world has not yet recognised, but she is finally starting to meet herself.

CHAPTER TWENTY-SIX

The Evolutionary Cycles of Diplomatic Identity

Becoming a Diplomat Through Cycles, Not Milestones

A woman does not become a diplomat in a single moment. She becomes one through slow, shifting, unannounced cycles that shape her more profoundly than any posting, promotion, or appointment ever could. Her evolution is not linear. It is layered, rhythmic, and quietly transformative.

As your document states, *"Her development is not linear; it is cyclical, layered, and characterised by a quiet evolution."*

She grows through experiences, losses, revelations, and endurance. Each cycle demands something different of her and offers its own form of wisdom.

The Cycle of Arrival

The first cycle is arrival, a phase marked by novelty, intensity, and overwhelm. In her earliest posting, she feels the tremor of stepping into a world at once exhilarating and intimidating. She learns quickly, absorbing not only the written rules but also the unwritten ones: how to read a room, interpret silences, and sense tension before it surfaces.

She learns to project confidence even when she feels uncertain.

She realises that diplomacy is not only about knowledge; it is about presence.

The Cycle of Proving

Then comes the cycle of proving. She feels compelled to demonstrate her competence, intelligence, and worth. She works longer hours, prepares more meticulously, and speaks with greater precision. She senses the scrutiny from colleagues, sceptics, and those quietly waiting for her to fail.

But she also discovers her resilience. She learns to turn doubt into fuel. She learns to meet scepticism with grace. She learns that she is stronger than she imagined.

The Cycle of Belonging

Eventually, belonging arrives. She begins to trust her instincts, her voice, and her judgement. She no longer performs confidence; she embodies it. She becomes a steady presence in the room, a source of clarity for others. She understands the rhythm of negotiations, the dance of influence, and the ebb and flow of diplomatic life.

Spaces that once intimidated her now feel familiar.

The Cycle of Stretching

But belonging is always followed by stretching, a cycle of greater responsibility, higher stakes, and deeper demands. Crises arise. Nights lengthen. Decisions weigh more heavily. She discovers the limits of her endurance, then surpasses them. She learns that leadership is not invulnerability. It is the ability to adapt without losing integrity. This cycle grows her in ways she never anticipated but desperately needed.

The Cycle of Questioning

Then comes the questioning, the cycle that tests her spirit. She wonders whether her sacrifices are worth it. She wonders whether she is losing too much of herself. She wonders whether anyone sees her humanity beneath the role.

This cycle forces her to confront fatigue, doubt, and a longing for a life that feels more balanced, more grounded, more authentically hers.

For Sofia, this cycle arrived quietly. One evening, after a long day of negotiations, she opened a message from an old friend: *"We miss you. You've changed."* She stared at the words, unsure whether they were meant with love or disappointment. She realised she no longer knew how to explain the woman she was becoming, not because she was ashamed, but because her evolution was unfolding in places no one could see.

She felt an ache, not for her old life, but for the version of herself she had abandoned without noticing. It was the first time she admitted she was tired, not of diplomacy, but of disappearing into it.

The Cycle of Return

The cycle of questioning eventually leads to return, a phase in which she begins to reclaim the parts of herself she had set aside. She rediscovers her voice, her softness, her joy. She remembers that she is not only a diplomat but a woman with a soul, a story, a body, and longing.

She practices self-recovery. She rebuilds her inner world. She learns to rest without guilt. She becomes whole again.

The Cycle of Becoming

Then, unexpectedly, comes becoming, the cycle in which everything she has learned, endured, and survived converges into a deeper version of herself. She leads with wisdom rather than fear, clarity rather than urgency, and presence rather than performance.

She recognises her true power, not the authority granted by titles, but the authority born of self-knowledge. She becomes the diplomat she was always meant to be.

The Rhythm of Her Becoming

These cycles do not follow a predictable order. They overlap, repeat, dissolve, and return. She may find herself proving long after she thought she belonged. She may question again after years of clarity. She may become anew more than once, each time deeper than before.

Her becoming is not a destination.
It is a rhythm.

As your document beautifully states, *"She becomes through cycles, each carving her, refining her, revealing her."*

The Diplomat the World Never Sees

For Minister Plenipotentiary Sofia Alvarez, these cycles became the true map of her career. She once believed her progression would be linear, from junior officer to senior diplomat, posting to posting, achievement to achievement. But she learned that her greatest growth came not from promotions but from the cycles that tested, unsettled, and transformed her.

One evening in Geneva, she sat by her apartment window, watching the city lights shimmer on the lake. She realised she was entering a new cycle, defined by clarity. She no longer needed to prove herself. She no longer feared being misunderstood. She no longer carried the weight of others' expectations.

She had become a woman who trusted her voice, honoured her boundaries, and recognised her worth. These cycles remain invisible to the world. They are not recorded in her biography, celebrated in ceremonies, or captured in photographs. Yet they shape her more profoundly than any external achievement ever could.

Becoming: a Lifelong Journey

In the end, she understands that her becoming is not something she completes.
It is something she lives.

Her identity is not fixed.
It is cyclical.
It is evolving.
It is alive.

And through each cycle, arrival, proving, belonging, stretching, questioning, returning, becoming, she discovers the quiet, powerful truth of her diplomatic journey:

Titles do not shape her.
She is shaped by transformation.

Lessons Learnt

Minister Plenipotentiary Sofia Alvarez's journey reveals that titles, promotions, or postings do not shape a diplomat; rather, it is the quiet, cyclical evolution within her. The chapter teaches that her identity is not formed in a single moment of achievement but through recurring phases of arrival, proving, belonging, stretching, questioning, returning, and becoming. Each cycle demands something different of her, whether courage, resilience, introspection, or surrender, and each cycle leaves her wiser, steadier, and more aligned with her true self.

She learns that arrival teaches humility, while proving teaches resilience, belonging fosters confidence, and stretching cultivates endurance. Questioning compels her to confront neglected aspects of herself, whereas returning restores her sense of humanity and reconnects her with her inner world. The process of becoming, the most profound cycle, reveals that her strength does not originate from external validation but from the clarity attained through transformation. These cycles do not follow a linear trajectory; they overlap, recur, dissolve, and reemerge, shaping her in ways no formal training could ever accomplish.

Ultimately, she discovers that her diplomatic identity is not a fixed construct but a living rhythm. She evolves not because the world demands it, but because her journey requires it. The chapter reveals that her true strength lies not in her ability to practise diplomacy, but in her willingness to be transformed by it. Through each cycle, she learns that her role does not define her; she is defined by her becoming. In that becoming, she uncovers the quiet truth of her leadership: she is shaped not by titles, but by transformation.

CHAPTER TWENTY-SEVEN

The Strategic Presence of Soft Power

The Quiet Force She Carries into Every Room

Soft power is often described as influence exercised without coercion, persuasion conducted without pressure, and presence manifested without assertion. However, for the female diplomat, soft power transcends mere theory; it constitutes the very landscape in which she operates daily. It represents the subtle force she brings to environments not inherently tailored for her, the quiet authority inherent in her voice, and the composed serenity she sustains even in turbulent circumstances.

Her presence may be understated, yet it remains unmistakably perceptible. It does not vociferate, yet it influences the ambience long before she articulates a word. It diminishes tension, enhances focus, and recalibrates a room's emotional climate with deliberate precision rather than by accident or passivity. For her, soft power is not indicative of weakness.

It is clarity.

It is a restraint.

It is mastery.

A Presence That Recalibrates the Room

On a winter morning in New York, Deputy Permanent Representative Aisha Rahman entered the Security Council chamber as a delicate layer of snow covered the city. Outside, the environment appeared subdued and delicate. The sky was tinted in shades of grey. Inside, however, the chamber was tense.

Delegates communicated in clipped tones, their postures stiff, their frustration evident. Recent developments had intensified the crisis overnight, leaving the room fragile and volatile, as if it might fracture under the pressure of conflicting narratives.

Aisha entered quietly, her steps deliberate, her expression composed. She did not raise her voice or make her presence conspicuous. Instead, she took her seat, opened her folder, and observed the room with calm attentiveness. Subsequently, an almost imperceptible transformation took place. The tone softened. The pace slowed. The atmosphere adjusted accordingly. Her steady, grounded presence subtly altered the room's emotional climate without a word.

This exemplifies her influence, characterised not by dominance but by steadiness; not by force but by presence; not by intimidation but by groundedness.

Empathy as Strategic Intelligence

For her, soft power is rooted in empathy. She listens not to respond but to understand. She observes not to judge but to discern. She speaks not to dominate but to illuminate. Her empathy is not sentimental; it is strategic. It enables her to sense emotional undercurrents, detect when a counterpart is posturing, when a delegation is wavering, and when compromise is possible. It enables her to build trust where it is scarce and to bridge divides across cultures, languages, and histories. Her credibility becomes her influence.

Her consistency becomes her leverage. Her reliability becomes her authority. People listen to her not because she demands it, but because she earns it. They trust her not because of her title, but because of her presence. They follow her not because she commands them, but because she inspires them.

The Courage to Remain Gentle

Yet soft power also requires courage, the courage to remain calm when others panic, to speak gently when others shout, and to hold her ground without raising her voice. Aisha found this courage in a moment she would never forget. During a tense negotiation, a senior delegate dismissed her intervention with a wave of his hand, speaking over her as though she were invisible. It was not the first time. It would not be the last. The room shifted uncomfortably, but no one intervened. Aisha felt the familiar sting, not of disrespect, but of the emotional labour required to remain composed. She waited. She breathed. She steadied herself. And when the moment returned, she spoke again, quietly, clearly, without a tremor. This time, the room listened.

Her soft power did not shield her from dismissal, but it ensured she was never erased.

Restraint as Discipline, Not Passivity

Soft power is not about being liked. It is about being respected. It is about being remembered. It is about being trusted. It is the influence that lingers after she leaves the room, the presence that shapes decisions long after the meeting ends, and the authority that does not announce itself yet cannot be ignored. Soft power is also a restraint. She does not react to provocation. She does not respond to disrespect with anger. She does not allow others to dictate her emotional landscape. Her restraint is not passivity; it is discipline, the discipline of choosing her moment, her tone, and her impact. Power is not always loud. Sometimes it is quiet, deliberate, and deeply felt.

Strength refined into influence.

Soft power is not effortless. It demands emotional labour, self-control, and constant calibration. Yet it remains her greatest strength. The woman who masters soft power becomes someone who shapes outcomes without raising her voice. She transforms rooms without demanding attention. She influences history without forcing her presence. Her soft power is not softness. It is a strength refined. Strength distilled. Strength embodied. Ultimately, she uncovers a profound truth: the world does not remember the loudest voice in the room; rather, it remembers the presence that changed the room.

Lessons Learnt

Soft power teaches her that influence need not be loud, authority need not be aggressive, and presence can be more transformative than force. She learns that empathy is a strategic asset, that restraint is a form of discipline, and that clarity can shift a room more effectively than volume. She discovers that courage is not always expressed through confrontation but often through composure. Above all, she realises that her greatest power lies not in how loudly she speaks but in how deeply she is felt.

CHAPTER TWENTY-EIGHT

The Things She Learns to Live Without

The Quiet Losses That Shape Her

There are aspects of the female diplomat's life that she gradually relinquishes, not by choice or desire, but because of the demands of her vocation. These absences do not arrive abruptly; they accumulate quietly, like shadows lengthening at dusk, subtle at first, then unmistakable. They shape her inner world as profoundly as her achievements. They become part of her narrative, her resilience, and the silent cost of her calling.

Living Without Certainty

She learns to accept the absence of certainty.

Diplomacy is a discipline built on shifting sands, where alliances shift without warning, crises erupt overnight, and decisions hinge on variables beyond her control.

She becomes fluent in ambiguity, making decisions with incomplete information and trusting her instincts when clarity is impossible. Certainty becomes a luxury she no longer expects.

She learns to dwell in the in-between, in the grey zones where truth is layered and outcomes remain perpetually unresolved.

Living Without Routine

She learns to live without routine. Her days are shaped by unpredictability, early-morning calls from the capital, late-night negotiations, sudden travel, and unforeseen crises. She adapts, recalibrates, and finds stability within chaos. Routine becomes something she observes in others' lives: neighbours walking their dogs at the same hour, families gathering for dinner, friends planning weekends months. Her life does not move in straight lines; it unfolds in spirals, waves, and unpredictable patterns.

Living Without Proximity

She learns to live without proximity. Distance becomes her constant companion, keeping her apart from home, family, and the familiar. She learns to love through screens, to celebrate milestones by message, and to grieve losses remotely. She holds her family in her heart when she cannot hold them in her arms. She adapts to the ache of absence, the quiet longing that lingers on long flights and in solitary evenings. Distance becomes the price she pays for the work she believes in.

Living Without Being Understood

She learns to live without being understood. The world sees her title, achievements, and composure. It does not see the emotional labour, the sacrifices, or the internal negotiations. She learns that few people truly grasp the complexity of her life, the weight of representation, the pressure of expectations, and the loneliness of leadership.

She carries her truth quietly, finding solace in the rare souls who see beyond the surface. Understanding becomes a gift, not a guarantee.

Living Without Rest

She learns to live without rest, not the rest of sleep, but the rest of the mind. Even on holidays, even at weekends, even in the quiet hours of the night, she remains tethered to responsibility. Her mind is always alert, always scanning, always ready. Rest becomes something she must fight for, fiercely protect, and learn to grant herself without guilt.

Living Without Belonging

She learns to live without the certainty of belonging. At every posting, she is both insider and outsider, welcomed yet observed, included yet evaluated. She learns to build community wherever she goes, to create a home in unfamiliar places, and to belong to the world without fully belonging anywhere.

Belonging becomes not a place but a practice, a way of anchoring herself in her own presence.

Living Without Emotional Collapse

She learns to live without emotional collapse, treating it as a luxury. She cannot break down in crises. She cannot unravel in front of her team. She cannot allow her emotions to spill into spaces that demand composure. She learns to maintain poise even when overwhelmed.

She learns to express grief privately, manage panic with controlled breathing, and compose herself before stepping into the public eye. Emotional collapse becomes a privilege she cannot afford.

Living Without the Illusion of Control

She learns to live without the illusion of control. Diplomacy teaches her to influence rather than dictate, to guide rather than command, to shape rather than guarantee. She releases her grip on outcomes, trusting the process even when it feels uncertain. Control becomes a myth she no longer chases.

The Loss That Changes Her

But the loss that shapes her most deeply is the one she never anticipated. One evening, at a reception in a foreign capital, she receives a message from her sister: a photo of their father in a hospital bed, smiling weakly, holding up a thumb. "He asked for you," the message reads.

She steps out into the cold night air, her breath trembling. She cannot leave. She cannot fly home. She cannot be there. She stands alone on the embassy terrace, the city lights blurring through her tears, realising that diplomacy has taught her to live without proximity, but it has never prepared her to live without moments she can never reclaim. Minutes later, she returns to the reception, composed and smiling, carrying a grief no one in the room can see.

The Things She Learns to Release

Yet there are also things she learns to live without that surprise her, things she once believed essential but now finds she can let go of. She learns to live without needing approval. She learns to live without fearing she will be underestimated. She learns to live without having to justify herself.

She stops apologising for her presence. She stops shrinking to make others comfortable. She stops explaining her choices to those who have not earned access to her truth.

The Woman She Becomes Through Loss

And in learning to live without these things, she discovers something profound: she is not diminished; she is distilled. She becomes sharper, clearer, more grounded, more herself. Because the things she learns to live without reveal what she cannot live without, namely her purpose, integrity, voice, and humanity, she finds the quiet truth of her journey: what she releases does not weaken her; it frees her.

Lessons Learnt

She learns that loss is not always depletion; sometimes it is refinement. She discovers that living without certainty strengthens her intuition, that living without routine sharpens her adaptability, and that living without proximity deepens her capacity for love. She realises that being misunderstood does not diminish her truth, that rest must be claimed rather than awaited, and that belonging begins within. S he understands that control is an illusion, but clarity is not. And she learns that the things she releases, namely approval, fear, and justification, are the very things that once held her back. In letting them go, she becomes more whole, not less.

CHAPTER TWENTY-NINE

The Hidden Self Behind Diplomatic Performance

The Woman and the Diplomat

The female diplomat must conceal aspects of her identity to perform her duties effectively, not out of shame or rejection, but because the society she serves is unprepared to accept her full humanity. The diplomatic environment demands a version of herself that is refined, composed, and resolute. It requires a woman who can withstand tension gracefully, assume responsibility without hesitation, and manage crises without revealing vulnerability. Consequently, she learns to hide facets of herself that do not conform to the expected image, such as softness, longing, tenderness, fatigue, and authenticity. She hides the woman who weeps easily, the woman who loves profoundly, the woman who feels intensely, the woman who quietly breaks, and the woman who needs rest and reassurance. She conceals her humanity.

The Performance the World Requires

Upon the arrival of Consul General Thandiwe Mbeki in Guangzhou amid a regional trade dispute, she quickly realised that the global perspective did not want her entire identity. Instead, it required the diplomat, strategist, negotiator, and representative. The expectation was for the version of herself capable of enduring twelve-hour meetings with resilience, responding to provocations with composure, and speaking authoritatively even amid uncertainty.

Furthermore, it demanded that the persona bear her nation's burden without revealing the weight on her shoulders. And so she concealed the woman who longed for home, yearned for her mother's voice, and wished she could curl beneath a blanket and exhale. She concealed the woman, overwhelmed by responsibility. She concealed herself because the world did not accommodate her needs.

Concealment as Discipline, Not Deception

Diplomacy demands discipline rather than deception. It requires managing her emotions, regulating her responses, and presenting a composed, measured, and controlled image. The woman she conceals does not signify weakness; she embodies the truth beneath the façade. She is the part of herself that bears the emotional burden of her responsibilities.

She conceals the woman who experiences fear, not because fear is shameful, but because it is often misinterpreted as incompetence.

She conceals the tired woman, not because fatigue equates to failure, but because it is seen as a sign of fragility. She conceals the sensitive woman, not because sensitivity is a flaw, but because it is often dismissed as instability.

She conceals the woman who longs to be embraced, not because longing is unprofessional, but because it is human. Human vulnerability is often deemed inconvenient in environments that demand neutrality.

The Strategy of Survival

Hiding herself is not erasure. It is a strategy.

It is survival.

The female diplomat conceals herself so the diplomat can function. She conceals the woman who suffers so the diplomat can endure. She conceals the woman who dreams so the diplomat can deliver. Yet the woman she conceals does not disappear. She waits. She watches. She breathes beneath the surface. She appears in the gentle light of early morning, before the world demands her voice, and in the quiet of late night, when the city hums outside her window. She emerges when she takes off her heels and exhales, when she wipes off her make-up and sees the fatigue in her eyes, when she sits alone in her apartment and finally allows herself to feel what she has suppressed throughout the day.

Self-Realization

Thandiwe experienced a moment of deep reflection one evening after an extensive negotiation session. The humidity hung in the air, and the city lights reflected on the Pearl River, resembling scattered gold. She stood by her window, her body weighed down by fatigue, her mind revisiting the day's confrontations. In that tranquillity, the woman she had concealed throughout the day emerged, the fatigued, solitary woman who yearned to be acknowledged beyond her professional title. She allowed herself to feel the pain, the longing, the truth. Taking a deep breath and straightening her posture, she realised that the woman she conceals is not a sign of weakness but rather her source of strength and stability.

The Woman Beneath the Diplomat

The concealed woman is the keeper of her empathy, the guardian of her intuition, the wellspring of her resilience. She is the part of her that refuses to be hardened by the world, the part that remembers her purpose, the part that insists on her humanity. The female diplomat learns that she must hide the woman she is to do the work, but she must never lose her. She must protect her. She must return to her. She must honour her. Because the woman she hides is the source of her strength.

And in the end, she discovers that the work does not require her to erase herself, only to sequence herself. The diplomat leads the world. The woman leads her soul. Both are necessary. Both are sacred. Both are hers.

Lessons Learnt

She learns that concealment is not betrayal but preservation. She discovers that the woman she hides is not a liability but a reservoir of truth, tenderness, and intuition. She realises that diplomacy demands composure, yet her humanity demands expression.

She understands that she can perform without losing herself and lead without abandoning the woman beneath the diplomat. And she learns that her strength does not come from the mask she wears, but from the woman she becomes when the mask is removed.

CHAPTER THIRTY

The Environments Not Created for Her Leadership

The Chamber

There are rooms that the female diplomat enters, built long before her arrival, that were shaped by histories that excluded her, governed by norms that resisted her, and arranged by traditions that did not imagine her presence. They carry the weight of old power, masculine, inherited, unquestioned. They bear the residue of decisions made by men who never needed to consider the possibility of a woman sitting at the table. Yet she enters them, sits, speaks, and shifts the atmosphere simply by being within their walls.

The Architecture of Exclusion

When Ambassador Rachael Ijor first entered the grand negotiation hall in Geneva, the air was cold with winter's chill. Snow clung to the edges of the tall windows, and the marble floors reflected the subdued morning light.

The chamber was magnificent yet undeniably antiquated in its architecture, rituals, and assumptions. The portraits adorning the walls were exclusively of men. The chairs were designed for broader shoulders. Microphones were positioned for deeper voices. The room retained a memory that did not include her. She perceived it immediately, the subtle tightening of the atmosphere, the quiet recalibration of the room as she took her seat. She observed the glances, the curiosity, the scepticism.

She sensed the unspoken question lingering like a shadow: Can she maintain this space? She did not respond verbally or through performance. She responded by simply existing.

The Silent Tests of Her Presence

The rooms, never intended for her, challenge her in ways invisible to others. They test her composure, her confidence, and her right to exist in spaces that once denied her. She learns to interpret these environments with precision, recognising the significance of seating arrangements that denote hierarchy, the side conversations that reveal alliances, and the tonal shifts that signal resistance. She becomes adept at recognising when her presence disturbs the established order, when her speech disrupts customary patterns, and when her authority challenges unspoken expectations. She learns to navigate these rooms not through aggression but through expertise.

The Quiet Defiance of Her Leadership

However, these chambers require something more profound; they demand that she comport herself with quiet defiance. Not loudly, nor confrontationally. Yet it must be undeniable. She must be twice as prepared, measured, and steady. She should anticipate the questions aimed at her, the doubts cast upon her, and the subsequent scrutiny. She must maintain her stance without hardening, assert herself without overcompensating, and articulate clearly without raising her voice. She must embody a balance that the room itself has never been required to learn.

There are moments when the environment seeks to diminish her through interruptions, dismissive tones, and subtle exclusions. She recognises the burden of these situations, yet remains unmoved. She understands that the environment is not neutral; it is shaped by history, power, and tradition. She also recognises that her presence is not an intrusion but an evolution.

The Moment She Reclaimed the Room

Rachael acquired this insight during a notably tense negotiation. A senior delegate repeatedly overshadowed her, his voice resounding throughout the table and obscuring her contributions. The attendees observed, awaiting her response, whether she would retreat or assert herself. She chose neither. Instead, she paused, awaited silence, and when it was achieved, she spoke with a composed demeanour that penetrated the chaos. Her words were intentional, her tone steadfast, and her presence unwavering. The atmosphere shifted; respect was realigned; influence was established. In that instant, she realised that the room was not originally designed for her, yet it could not operate effectively without her.

The Weight and Worth of Her Presence

Diplomacy also reveals a profound truth: the silent resilience of her existence. Her presence becomes a declaration. Her voice becomes disruptive. Her competence challenges assumptions. Her leadership redefines what is possible. Nevertheless, these spaces also diminish her resources. They exhaust her energy and necessitate emotional labour. They demand continual vigilance to navigate environments that challenge her legitimacy.

Nevertheless, she endures, not because the spaces are accommodating, but because they must be transformed. Not because the spaces are comfortable, but because they must be confronted. Not because the spaces are prepared for her, but because the world is.

The Night She Understood Her Purpose

One evening, after a long day of negotiations, Rachael stepped out into the Geneva night. Snowflakes drifted gently around her, settling on her coat like quiet blessings. She realised the rooms she entered were not meant to remain static. Her presence was essential to their evolution. Her voice played a role in their rewriting. Her journey served as a catalyst for their transformation. The rooms never designed for her became spaces she redefined, not through coercion, but through consistent presence; not through confrontation, but through steady perseverance; not through rebellion, but through resilience.

The Legacy She Leaves Behind

Ultimately, she realised that the rooms which once resisted her would one day accommodate future women, not because the rooms themselves changed, but because she had. Her presence carved out space where none had existed. Her leadership softened the rigidity of old structures. Her resilience expanded the boundaries of what was possible. And her courage ensured that the next woman who entered would not feel like an anomaly, but a continuation.

Lessons Learned

Rachael learns that diplomatic environments are not barriers but battlegrounds for transformation. She discovers that her presence alone disrupts old patterns, that her voice recalibrates expectations, and that her leadership redefines the architecture of power. She realises that resistance is not a sign of her inadequacy but evidence of her impact. And she understands that the rooms built without her are precisely the rooms that need her most.

Through her persistence, she becomes not only a participant in these spaces but also a force that reshapes them for those who will follow.

CHAPTER THIRTY-ONE

The Identity Shift Required by Diplomatic Departure

The City That Softened Her Edges

On her first morning in the capital, Ambassador Hana Sato stepped out of her residence and felt the warmth settle on her skin like an unfamiliar kindness. The air carried the scent of ripe fruit and early rain, a stark contrast to the crisp, disciplined mornings in Kyoto. The city moved with a rhythm she did not yet understand, unhurried, expressive, and alive in ways that unsettled her quiet precision.

She moved slowly, immersing herself in the colours, sounds, and the vibrant rhythm of a place that seemed to breathe in a distinctive way. Vendors arranged their stalls with natural ease. Children in bright uniforms darted between vehicles. A woman swept her storefront while humming a tune unfamiliar to Hana. Hana paused at a small roundabout where jacaranda trees framed the sky in gentle purple hues. She sensed the city observing her with subtlety, as if inviting her to relax the stiffness she had carried for years from disciplined diplomacy. She was unaware that this place would reform her, soften her edges, deepen her empathy, and compel a form of vulnerability she had long concealed.

The Realisation

Three years later, standing beneath the same jacaranda trees, she realised she had to leave. The city she once observed with caution had become a place she understood instinctively, with its silences, its tensions, and its unspoken rules.

She knew which streets held morning calm, which cafés offered refuge after long days, which diplomatic corridors required firmness, and which required grace. And that was precisely when departure arrived.

It always came when she was finally rooted.

Her first crisis emerged sharply: the crisis of professional uprooting, the demand to abandon influence just as it was solidifying.

The Discipline of Leaving

Hana had learned that departure was not a logistical task but a discipline of diplomatic life. She left cities just as she mastered their rhythm, parted with friendships just as they deepened, and abandoned routines just as they became stabilising anchors.

She never left because she was restless.

She left because duty demanded movement.

Each departure required her to dismantle a life she had built with care, folding away memories with the same precision she used to fold her suits, deliberate, controlled, and quietly painful.

The Rupture Beneath the Ritual

Leaving was never a simple relocation. For Hana, it was rupture, a subtle unravelling of a life woven into its surroundings. During her final week, she conducted the traditional **farewell courtesy call** to the Foreign Ministry.

The polished smiles, expressions of formal gratitude, and the ceremonial exchange of gifts all concealed the truth that she was relinquishing a life she had meticulously constructed. The cafés where she composed policy briefs, the corridors where she negotiated delicate compromises, and the riverbanks where she paused after long days all became silent witnesses to her impending departure.

The People and Selves She Must Release

Hana learned to let go of colleagues who had become confidants, neighbours who had become companions, and routines that had provided stability. Yet the most profound release was internal. She had to let go of the woman she had become in this city, the version of herself forged by its climate, demands, and cultural rhythm. She departs without unravelling. She loosens her grip without losing her identity.

She advances without erasing the history she bears.

The Moment That Broke Her Quietly

What no one saw was the moment she returned to her residence after her final courtesy call. Her housekeeper had placed a small bouquet of jacaranda blossoms on her dining table, a gesture of farewell, gratitude, and affection. Hana stood there, staring at the flowers, feeling the weight of everything she was leaving behind.

The friendships.

The routines.

The version of herself she had grown into. She touched one of the petals, and it fell softly onto her palm. It was the kind of moment that quietly breaks a diplomat.

The kind of moment she carries into every negotiation afterwards.

The Rebuilding That Follows

Yet she rebuilds. Departure is not only a loss; it is renewal. It is the shedding of one season and the beginning of another. It is the chance to rediscover herself in a new landscape. At each new posting, Hana reconstructs her identity piece by piece, not replicating what she left behind but allowing herself to evolve. She learns that home is not a location but a presence she carries. Her identity is not defined by where she serves but by who she becomes.

The Evolution Hidden Within Leaving

Her second crisis emerges quietly yet powerfully: the crisis of internal identity reconstruction, the tension between who she was at her last posting and who she must become at the next. The shift demanded by diplomatic departure is not about avoiding pain; it is about honouring it. It is about allowing the ache to coexist with anticipation, trusting that what she leaves behind remains part of her even as she steps into the unknown.

Leaving is not abandonment.
It is evolution.
Not erasure, but expansion.
Not loss, but transformation.

Ultimately, Hana recognises that the woman capable of leaving without breaking is not the one who feels nothing, but the one who feels deeply and moves forward. Her life is not defined by the places she leaves behind, but by the resilience she carries into every new beginning.

Lessons Learnt

She learns that departure is not a failure of attachment but a testament to her capacity for renewal.
She discovers that leaving does not diminish the life she built; it deepens it.
She realises that identity is not fixed to geography but shaped by movement, memory, and meaning.
And she understands that the courage to depart is not the absence of sorrow but the willingness to carry it with grace into the next chapter of her becoming.

CHAPTER THIRTY-TWO

The Unvoiced Realities of Her Professional Identity

Unspoken Truth

The professional identity of the female diplomat is shaped not only by the responsibilities she bears but also by the truths she must conceal. These truths do not stem from weakness or uncertainty; they arise from the complex interplay of duty, perception, and the unspoken expectations that govern her world. She operates in environments where vulnerability is misread, where honesty is politicised, and where silence becomes both armour and strategy. Her identity is therefore constructed not only by what she articulates but also by what she must withhold.

There are truths she cannot speak aloud, not because she lacks courage, but because the world is unprepared to receive them. They lie beneath her professionalism, beneath her composure, beneath the carefully measured statements she delivers. They shape her decisions, sharpen her humanity, and deepen her resilience, yet they remain unspoken, held within the quiet chambers of her mind. Her silence is not emptiness; it is a form of discernment, a recognition that diplomacy often demands restraint over revelation.

The Exhaustion She Cannot Admit

One of the most profound truths she cannot voice is the depth of her exhaustion. It is not the kind of tiredness that sleep cures, but a bone-deep fatigue that settles after years of carrying responsibility without pause. She cannot admit that she feels isolated, even in crowded rooms, even among colleagues, even with a calendar full of engagements. She cannot confess that the work overwhelms her in the quiet intervals between crises, when the world assumes she is strongest. To acknowledge such exhaustion would risk being perceived as incapable, even though her endurance far exceeds what is visible.

Doubts and Longings

She also carries doubts she must bear alone. She cannot voice her fear of failure, her longing to withdraw, or her desire for gentleness in a profession that rewards hardness. She cannot say she sometimes feels like an imposter, not because she lacks competence, but because the room was never designed for her. She cannot say she carries the weight of representation, that every mistake feels amplified, every success scrutinised, and every decision a test she cannot afford to fail. Her silence becomes a shield against misinterpretation, a way of protecting her legitimacy in spaces where her presence is still contested.

There is also a longing she cannot express. She cannot say she envies those whose lives are not shaped by urgency, whose days are not dictated by crises, and whose identities are not bound to national expectation. She cannot say she longs for a life where she is supported rather than always supporting, where she can rest rather than perform strength, and where she can be vulnerable without consequence. She cannot say she misses the version of herself that existed before the world demanded so much.

These longings do not diminish her commitment; they reveal the humanity that sustains it.

Moments of Silence

Her silence is not a void; it is a boundary. It protects her from a world that often misunderstands the emotional labour embedded in diplomacy. It shields her from scrutiny that would distort her truth. It allows her to maintain the composure needed to navigate complex political landscapes. Diplomacy values steadiness over confession, restraint over vulnerability, and composure over candour. And so she learns to speak in layers: the official truth, the strategic truth, the diplomatic truth. The personal truth remains unspoken, held close, honoured privately.

Yet there are moments when she allows herself to be recognised. Not relief. Not resolution. But recognition. In the quiet of her own space, she whispers the truths she cannot say aloud, acknowledging her fatigue, her doubts, her longing, and her humanity. In that private honesty, she discovers that silence is not denial. It is survival. It is the space where she gathers strength, reclaims her identity, and remembers that she is more than the expectations placed upon her.

The Strength Hidden in Her Silence

The unvoiced realities of her professional identity do not weaken her; they fortify her. They remind her that her strength is measured not by what she reveals to the world, but by what she carries with grace. Her silence is not a sign of fragility but a testament to her discernment. It is the quiet architecture of her resilience, the foundation of her diplomatic presence. Ultimately, her life is shaped not only by the truths she speaks, but by the truths she holds—truths that deepen her humanity, sharpen her clarity, and reveal the depth of her professional courage.

Lessons Learnt

She learns that silence is not emptiness but intention.
She discovers that the truths she withholds are not signs of fragility but evidence of discernment.
She realises that her unspoken realities do not weaken her professionalism; they fortify it.
And she understands that her strength is not measured by what she reveals to the world, but by what she carries with grace in the privacy of her soul.

CHAPTER THIRTY-THREE

The Inheritance She Carries

The Legacy

The morning light in Stockholm rose slowly, stretching across the frozen river like a quiet invocation. Ambassador Nura El-Mahdi stood by her window, watching the city wake beneath a pale Scandinavian sky. The cold pressed gently against the glass, a stark contrast to the warm, dust-scented dawns of Khartoum, where her earliest memories lived.

As she wrapped her shawl around her shoulders, she felt the presence of the women who shaped her: her grandmother's steady gaze, her mother's unspoken sacrifices, her aunt's whispered prayers. They travelled with her across continents, postings, and the shifting terrain of diplomacy. She did not enter this city alone. She entered carrying a lineage.

This inheritance was not recorded in legal documents, nor passed down through ceremonial rites. It comprised history, expectation, sacrifice, and lineage, a legacy shaped by women who were silenced, excluded, or confined to rooms they were never permitted to enter. It was also the inheritance of her family, her culture, and her nation: whispered stories, burdens borne in silence, dreams deferred but never extinguished.

This inheritance was not material. It was emotional, psychological, and spiritual.

The Lineage That Enters the Room Before She Speaks

Later that afternoon, she sat opposite a panel of European counterparts as they negotiated a humanitarian corridor agreement. The stakes were high, the atmosphere taut with political tension. A senior official leaned forward, his tone clipped as he said, "Ambassador, your government must demonstrate stronger internal alignment." It was a challenge wrapped in diplomacy, a test of her composure, a provocation she was expected to absorb without flinching.

Nura inhaled slowly, grounding herself in the memory of her grandmother's voice, the one that had carried her through childhood: strength is not the absence of pressure; it is the refusal to be reshaped by it. When she spoke, her voice was steady. "Assurance is not a declaration; it is a commitment. Sudan is committed. Let us focus on the mechanisms that make this corridor viable." The room shifted.

The tension eased. Her inheritance steadied her hand. Her lineage entered the room before she spoke and remained long after the meeting ended.

Her inheritance was resilience, the understanding that her presence in these spaces was intentional and hard-earned. It was a sacrifice, the awareness that her opportunities were built on the labour of those who came before her. It was hope, the conviction that her presence widened the path for those who would follow. But it was also an expectation: to excel, to represent, and to succeed not only for herself but also for her family, her community, and her nation.

The Expectation That Lives in Silence

That evening, she returned to her apartment overlooking the river. As she took off her coat, a small embroidered cloth slipped from her pocket, a keepsake her mother had tucked into her luggage before she left Sudan. She held it gently, tracing the familiar patterns stitched by women in her family for generations. Patterns of survival. Patterns of memory. Patterns of hope.

In that quiet moment, she felt the weight of all she carried: the dreams her grandmother never lived to see, the education her mother fought to access, the opportunities denied to generations of Sudanese women. Her inheritance was not a burden. It was a summons.

The expectation she carried was rarely spoken aloud, yet it was always felt. It lived in the quiet messages from home that said, " *We are proud of you.*

It lived in the eyes of young women who saw her as proof that their aspirations were possible.

It lived in the unspoken belief that she must not fail, for her failure would be read as collective.

She carried the legacy of silence, the silence imposed on women who were not permitted to speak, whose brilliance was overlooked and whose potential was constrained. She carried their unspoken narratives, their unrealised ambitions, their quiet endurance. She became the voice they were denied, the presence they were refused, and the embodiment of the possibilities they never lived to see.

The Cultural Memory

She carried cultural memory, the rituals, values, and wisdom passed down through generations. The proverbs whispered by her grandmother, the prayers taught by her mother, and the resilience embedded in her lineage. These became her compass in unfamiliar rooms, her grounding in foreign landscapes, and her anchor in moments of uncertainty. Yet alongside this strength, she also carried the legacy of suffering, the pain of historical marginalisation, the strain of intergenerational adversity, and the loneliness of being the first.

She held the emotional remnants of battles fought long before her birth. She knew that her existence was both a triumph and a testament to the long journey that made her possible.

Her professional crisis unfolded against the backdrop of every negotiation. She was expected to represent a nation in transition, one whose internal fractures were often projected onto her. Every hesitation felt magnified. Every success felt conditional. Her personal crisis ran parallel to it. She longed for home, not the geography, but the women whose stories shaped her. She wondered whether she was honouring them or drifting too far from the life they had imagined. Diplomacy demanded movement. Inheritance demanded memory. She lived in the tension between them.

The Inheritance That Reveals Itself in Stillness

One night, after a long week of negotiations, she received a voice note from her younger sister. "Nura, when I see you in these rooms, I see all of us. You carry us with dignity." She listened to it twice, then a third time.

Pride swelled in her chest, but so did a sharp ache, the ache of knowing her success was not entirely her own. It belonged to women who never had the chance to stand where she stood.

A single tear slipped down her cheek. Not from sadness, but from recognition. It was the kind of moment that quietly breaks a diplomat, the kind she carries into every room after.

In the stillness that followed, her inheritance revealed itself with greater clarity. She realised that her achievements were not hers alone; they belonged to a lineage that stretched behind her and extended beyond her. Inheritance, she understood, is not simply what is passed down; it is what is carried forward. It is not the stories told, but the stories lived. It is not the weight of expectation, but the architecture of identity. A woman does not inherit history; she inherits unfinished work.

The female diplomat does not merely step into history; she continues a sentence that began long before her and will outlive her.

The Legacy She Will One Day Pass On

As she prepared for another day of negotiations, Nura stood once more by the window, watching the river's slow flow beneath the winter light. She whispered softly into the quiet room, "I am because they endured." In that moment, she understood that the inheritance she carried was not something she bore; it was something she embodied. It was the quiet force behind her voice, the steady fire beneath her composure, and the legacy she would one day pass on.

She was not merely a diplomat; she was a continuation, a bridge, a living testament to the resilience of the women who shaped her. Her presence in diplomatic spaces was not accidental; it was ancestral. Her life was not only a personal journey but a collective unfolding of histories, sacrifices, and hopes converging in her.

She learns that her inheritance is not a weight but a lineage of strength. She discovers that the stories she carries are not burdens but blueprints. She realises that her presence in diplomatic spaces is not accidental but ancestral. And she understands that the legacy she embodies is not merely inherited; it is expanded, refined, and prepared for those who will follow her path.

Lessons Learnt

She learns that her inheritance is not a weight but a lineage of strength, a quiet architecture of identity built long before her birth. She discovers that the stories she carries are not burdens but blueprints, guiding her through rooms her foremothers were never permitted to enter. She realises that her presence in diplomatic spaces is not accidental but ancestral, the culmination of sacrifices that shaped her long before she understood their meaning. And she understands that the legacy she embodies is not merely inherited; it is expanded, refined, and prepared for the women who will one day walk further than she was ever allowed to.

CHAPTER THIRTY-FOUR

The Emotional Cartography of Her Diplomatic Journey

Marked Places

The fog rolled gently over Maputo at dawn, softening the city's edges as Ambassador Helena Duarte stepped onto her balcony. The air carried the scent of salt and woodsmoke, a blend that reminded her of childhood mornings in Porto, though the warmth here wrapped around her like a quiet insistence. She watched fishermen push their boats into the water, their silhouettes moving with a rhythm older than diplomacy itself. In that stillness, she experienced it once more, an enduring truth she had discovered across various continents: certain places visited by a diplomat from which one never truly returns.

These places imprint themselves on her internal landscape, altering the architecture of her identity in ways she cannot always articulate. They become coordinates on her emotional map, quiet markers that shape her intuition, leadership, and understanding of the world.

They are not always dramatic.

They are not always beautiful. They are not always easy. But they become part of her. Some places change her because of what she has witnessed. Some because of what she survived. Some because of what she learned about herself. Some because of what she lost.

Some because of what she found.

The Places Where Resilience Lives

Her first week in Mozambique brought her to a coastal community recovering from a devastating cyclone. The air carried the scent of sea salt and smoke; the streets pulsed with life even as they bore the scars of destruction. Children played barefoot among the ruins. Women swept debris from the entrances of homes that no longer had roofs. Men repaired fishing nets with quiet determination.

Helena met a mother who offered her tea despite having lost everything. She met a volunteer who worked through the night without complaint. She met an elder who gave directions with dignity even as his home lay in ruins. These encounters etched themselves into her emotional cartography. They taught her that resilience is not a performance; it is a way of being. They taught her that humanity endures even in the shadow of loss. They taught her that the world's most profound lessons are often delivered in whispers, not declarations.

Lessons on Fragility and Strength

Other postings gave her insights into fragility, the vulnerability of systems, peace, and human life. In Geneva, she observed how quickly diplomatic consensus could fracture. In Beirut, she recognised the precarious nature of safety. In Jakarta, she experienced how quickly political landscapes could shift unexpectedly. Nonetheless, these locations also imparted lessons in strength, community resilience, the bravery of women, and the persistence of hope. They conveyed the importance of understanding limits, including personal boundaries, the constraints inherent in diplomacy, and the sobering reality that not every crisis is resolvable. Furthermore, they illuminated the possibilities for healing, reconstruction, and renewal.

The Sites of Remembrance

But some places diminished her vitality. Places where she witnessed suffering, she could not unsee. Places where she confronted the limits of her influence. Places where she carried the weight of decisions that did not yield perfect outcomes. Places where she learned that leadership is often a negotiation with her own conscience.

She never returned from the place where she first realised the world is unfair in ways that cannot be negotiated. She never returned from the place where she learned that leadership sometimes requires choosing the lesser of two imperfect options. She never returned from the place where she saw the cost of conflict reflected in a child's eyes. She never returned from the place where she discovered her breaking point, and the strength that rose after. These places left marks not visible but deep. They shaped her empathy. They sharpened her judgement. They deepened her humanity.

The Places That Restore Her

Yet some places restored her. The quiet village in the Swiss Alps where she learned to breathe again. The coastal town in Cape Verde, where the rhythm of the waves reminded her of joy. The bustling market in Bangkok, where she felt alive in the chaos. The snowy street in Warsaw, where she realised she was stronger than she believed. These places became part of her healing, part of her memory, part of her becoming.

The Moment of Realisation

She realised, often in a moment of stillness, perhaps on a balcony overlooking a city at dusk, or in the hush of early morning before the world awakened, that she would never fully leave certain places behind. A part of her remained anchored in the resilience she witnessed, the humanity she encountered, and the lessons she absorbed. The places her heart never returns from are not merely geographic. They are emotional. They are psychological. They are transformative. They are the places where she grew, where she broke, where she healed, where she awakened.

And in the end, she understood that she did not simply travel through the world. The world travelled through her. The diplomat does not map the world; the world maps her. The emotional cartography she carries becomes the quiet atlas of her leadership.

Lessons Learnt

She learns that every place she serves becomes part of her internal landscape, shaping her in ways no training manual could anticipate. She discovers that resilience is not taught but witnessed, that fragility and strength coexist, and that some lessons can be learned only through presence. She realises that the places that wound her also deepen her, and the places that restore her also rebuild her. And she understands that her diplomatic journey is not only geographic; it is emotional, a map drawn not on paper but on the soul.

CHAPTER THIRTY-FIVE

The Emotional Cartography of Her Diplomatic Journey

When the World Begins to Map Her

Some places imprint themselves on a diplomat's inner landscape, altering the architecture of her identity in ways she cannot always articulate. They become coordinates on her emotional map, quiet markers that shape her intuition, leadership, and understanding of the world. They are not always dramatic. They are not always beautiful. They are not always easy. But they become part of her.

At dawn in Maputo, the fog rolled gently over the city, softening its edges as Ambassador Helena Duarte stepped onto her balcony. The air carried the scent of salt and woodsmoke, a mixture that reminded her of childhood mornings in Porto, though the warmth here wrapped around her like a quiet insistence. She wrapped her shawl around her shoulders and leaned on the railing, watching fishermen push their boats into the water, their silhouettes moving with a rhythm older than diplomacy itself.

Below, the city was waking slowly, a woman sweeping her doorstep, a boy chasing a chicken across the road, a vendor arranging mangoes in a neat pyramid. The world was ordinary and extraordinary at once.

And in that stillness, Helena felt it again, the truth she had learned across continents:

The diplomat does not simply travel through the world; the world travels through her.

Every posting, every crisis, every community, every landscape leaves a mark.
Her emotional cartography is not a record of where she has been, but of who she became there.

The Places Where Resilience Lives

Helena's first week in Mozambique brought her to a coastal community recovering from a devastating cyclone. The drive there took hours, long stretches of road lined with palm trees bent by the storm, roofs torn from houses, and fields where crops lay flattened like defeated soldiers.

When she arrived, the air carried the scent of sea salt and smoke; the streets pulsed with life even as they bore the scars of destruction. Children played barefoot among broken walls, their laughter rising above the rubble. Women swept debris from the entrances of homes that no longer had roofs. Men repaired fishing nets with quiet determination, their hands moving with the muscle memory of generations.

Helena walked through the community with a local volunteer named Amélia, who spoke softly but moved with purpose.

"People think resilience is loud," Amélia said, stepping over a fallen beam. "But here, it is quiet. It is in the way we wake up the next day."

Helena nodded, absorbing the truth in her words. She met a mother who offered her tea despite losing everything. The woman's hands trembled slightly as she poured, but her voice was steady.

"We start again," she said. "There is no other choice."

She met a volunteer who worked through the night without complaint, his eyes red but his spirit unbroken.

"We rebuild," he said. "Not because we are strong, but because we must be."

She met an elder who gave directions with dignity even as his home lay in ruins.

"This is where the school used to be," he said, pointing to a pile of bricks. "We will build it again."

These encounters etched themselves into her emotional cartography.
They taught her that resilience is not a performance; it is a way of being.
They taught her that humanity persists even in the shadow of loss.
They taught her that the world's most profound lessons are often delivered in whispers, not declarations.

Lessons on Fragility and Strength

Other postings taught her about fragility, the vulnerability of systems, of peace, of human life.

In Geneva, she learned how quickly diplomatic consensus could fracture. She remembered one night vividly, a negotiation that stretched past midnight, the room thick with tension. Delegates argued over a single clause, each word carrying the weight of national pride. She watched alliances crumble in real time, watched tempers flare, watched the illusion of stability dissolve like sugar in hot water.

During a break, she stepped into the hallway, leaning against the cool marble wall. A colleague approached her.

“You look tired,” he said.

“I’m not tired,” she replied. “I’m witnessing how fragile peace really is.”

In Beirut, she discovered the fragility of safety, recalling the distant sound of an explosion that reverberated through the windows of her residence. She paused, breath caught, before her training prompted her to act. She attended to her staff, contacted the mission, and assessed the situation. Yet that night, as she lay in bed, she felt the weight of vulnerability settling into her bones.

In Jakarta, she realised how quickly political environments could shift.

One morning, she was awakened by news that a coalition had disintegrated overnight. Meetings were cancelled, alliances reconfigured, and strategies revised. She devoted the day to navigating this uncertainty, her mind racing to keep pace with rapidly unfolding events that defied immediate analysis.

Nevertheless, these locations also imparted lessons about resilience, community perseverance, women's bravery, and the persistence of hope. They taught her about her limitations, her personal boundaries, the constraints inherent in diplomacy, and the sobering reality that not all crises are resolvable. Moreover, they illuminated the potential for healing, reconstruction, and renewal.

These places became symbolic thresholds, points at which she confronted the tension between the aspirations of diplomacy and the often-restrictive realities of the world.

The Places That Diminish Her Vitality

But some places diminished her vitality. Places where she witnessed suffering, she could not unsee.
Places where she confronted the limits of her influence.
Places where she carried the weight of decisions with imperfect outcomes.
Places where she learned that leadership is often a negotiation with her own conscience.

She remembered one such place, a refugee camp on the outskirts of a conflict zone. The air was thick with dust and despair. Children lined up for water, their eyes too old for their faces. A mother clutched her baby, her voice breaking as she spoke.

"Will anyone help us?" she asked.

Helena swallowed hard.
She wanted to say yes.
She wanted to promise safety, shelter, certainty.
But diplomacy does not deal in promises; it deals only in possibilities.

She never returned from the place where she first realised that the world is inherently unjust in ways that cannot be rectified. She never returned from the place where she understood that leadership occasionally necessitates choosing the lesser of two flawed alternatives. She never returned from the place where she observed the toll of conflict mirrored in a child's eyes.

She never returned from the experience in which she identified her breaking point and the resilience that emerged thereafter.

These places left marks not visible, but deep.

They shaped her empathy.

They sharpened her judgment.

They deepened her humanity.

The Places That Restore Her

Yet some places restored her. The quiet village in the Swiss Alps where she learned to breathe again. She remembered walking along a snow-covered path, the air crisp, the silence profound. For the first time in months, her shoulders dropped, her breath deepened, her mind quietened.

The coastal town in Cape Verde, where the rhythm of the waves reminded her of joy. She spent evenings on the sand, watching fishermen mend their nets, listening to the ocean's steady heartbeat.

The bustling market in Bangkok, where she felt alive in the chaos. Vendors calling out prices, spices perfuming the air, colours exploding in every direction, it reminded her that the world was vast, vibrant, and endlessly surprising.

The snowy street in Warsaw, where she realised she was stronger than she had believed. She had arrived exhausted, weighed down by a difficult posting. But one morning, as she walked to the mission through falling snow, something shifted inside her, a quiet resilience rising from a place she thought was empty.

These places became part of her healing, part of her memory, part of her becoming. They were not escapes; they were recalibrations.

They reminded her that the diplomat's life is not only defined by crisis, but also by the moments that return her to herself.

The Moment She Understands What She Carries

It happened one evening in Maputo, long after the city had surrendered to night. Helena stood on her balcony, the air warm against her skin, the distant sound of waves folding into the shore. The lights of the city shimmered like scattered stars, and somewhere below, a radio played a soft, melancholic melody.

She closed her eyes, and for a moment, she felt the weight of every place she had ever served.

Geneva's cold precision.
Beirut's trembling resilience.
Jakarta's restless energy.
Cape Verde's healing quiet.
Warsaw's unexpected strength.
Mozambique's unbroken hope.

She realised then that she would never completely leave certain places behind. A part of her remained anchored in the resilience she witnessed, the humanity she encountered, the lessons she absorbed. The places her heart never returns to are not merely geographic.
They are emotional.
They are psychological.
They are transformative.

They are the places where she grew, where she broke, where she healed, where she awakened.

And in that moment, she understood the truth she had carried for years without naming it:

The diplomat does not map the world; the world maps her.
And the emotional cartography she carries becomes the quiet atlas of her leadership.

Lessons Learnt

She learns that every place she serves becomes part of her internal landscape, shaping her in ways no training manual could anticipate. She discovers that resilience is not taught but witnessed, that fragility and strength coexist, and that some lessons can be learned only through presence. She realises that the places that wound her also deepen her, and the places that restore her also rebuild her.

Helena understands that her diplomatic journey is not only geographic; it is emotional, a map drawn not on paper but on the soul.

CHAPTER THIRTY-SIX

The Quiet Maturity That Emerges from Diplomatic Seasons

When Maturity Arrives Without Announcement

The first snowfall of the year gently settled over Helsinki, like a silent benediction, in the embassy courtyard. Ambassador Keziah Mwangi paused beneath the subdued winter sky, her breath forming small clouds as she watched the city awaken, its movements slow and deliberate. The cold pressed against her cheeks, offering a stark contrast to the warm Nairobi mornings she once took for granted.

She adjusted her scarf and stood for a moment, listening to the muffled hush that winter's arrival brings, a silence that was not vacant but full. A silence that provided space for contemplation. A silence that uncovered what noise often concealed.

In that tranquillity, she sensed something intangible at first, a steadiness that had not always been present.

Maturity had not manifested suddenly for her. It arrived through a quiet accumulation of seasons: each posting, each crisis, each departure, each return, each leaving a mark upon her. This maturity was shaped not by chronological age, but by exposure; not by hierarchical rank, but by experience; not by titles, but by internal shifts that occur when a woman has experienced enough cycles of the world to discern its patterns.

It was subtle.
It did not announce itself.
It settled into her gradually, like dawn light entering a room.

The Maturity That Changes How She Listens

Later that morning, she sat opposite a delegation negotiating a sensitive security arrangement. The room was warm, the air thick with competing agendas. A pot of coffee steamed in the corner, untouched. Papers rustled. Pens clicked. Tension hung like a low-hanging cloud.

Years ago, she might have rushed to fill the silence, eager to prove her competence, assert her presence, and demonstrate that she belonged in the room. But now she listened, fully and patiently, without the urgency that once drove her. A delegate from the host country leaned forward, frustration tightening his jaw.

"Ambassador Mwangi, your position is unclear," he said. "We need a definitive answer."

She did not flinch.
She did not rush.
She did not allow the pressure to dictate her pace.

Instead, she observed him, noting how his fingers tapped the table, how his eyes darted to his colleagues, how his voice carried more anxiety than aggression. She understood what was said. But she also understood what was withheld.

When she finally spoke, her words were fewer, her tone measured, her clarity unmistakable.

"Our position is clear," she said softly. "But clarity does not require haste."

The room shifted.
The tension eased.
The conversation recalibrated.

She had learned that not every battle required her sword, not every provocation her reaction, not every crisis her panic. She had learned to distinguish between what was urgent and what was important, between what was noise and what was signal, between what was personal and what was structural.

Leadership, she realised, was not performance.
It was presence.

The Maturity That Changes How She Responds

That afternoon, she received a message from her capital, a critique of her recent briefing. The tone was sharp, the feedback blunt. Years earlier, such a message would have unsettled her. She would have replayed every sentence she had spoken, every gesture she had made, every decision she had taken.

But now, she read the message once.
Then she placed her phone on her desk.
Then she breathed.

Her aide, a young officer named Elias, hesitantly entered the room.

"Ambassador… are you alright?" he asked.

She smiled, not the diplomatic smile she wore in public, but a genuine one.

"I'm fine," she said. "Criticism is information, not identity."

Elias blinked, surprised.
He had expected defensiveness.
He had expected tension.
He had expected the emotional turbulence he had seen in other leaders.

But she had learned something essential: Maturity is not the absence of emotion. It is the mastery of emotion.

She no longer met tension with urgency but with steadiness.
She no longer met criticism with defensiveness but with clarity.
She no longer met uncertainty with fear but with perspective.

Her responses had changed because she had changed.

Seasons of Pressure

There had been seasons that shaped her, seasons of loneliness, transition, doubt, pressure, and reinvention. She remembered one winter evening from her first posting, years ago. She had been overwhelmed, exhausted, and convinced she was failing. She had sat on the floor of her flat, surrounded by briefing papers, tears slipping down her cheeks.

"I can't do this," she had whispered into the empty room.

But she had done it.
She had survived that season.
And the next.
And the next.

Now, standing in Helsinki years later, she understood that those seasons had not hardened her; they had refined her. They had taught her resilience, but also softness. They had taught her strength, but also surrender. They had taught her strategy, but also stillness.

She had become a different woman from the one who had first entered the service, not harder but wiser; not colder but clearer; not detached but discerning. She carried herself differently now, not because she had altered her posture, but because she had shifted her centre.

The Moment She Realises She Has Changed

One evening, after a long day of meetings, she returned to her residence overlooking the frozen harbour. The sky was a deep indigo, the water below a sheet of dark glass. She removed her coat, hung it on the rack, and caught her reflection in the hallway mirror.

She paused.

Something in her posture, her eyes, the quiet confidence of her stance made her look twice. She stepped closer, studying the woman in the mirror.

She realised she no longer reacted to the world as she once had.
The things that once unsettled her now passed through her with less turbulence. The opinions that once defined her now held less sway. The expectations that

once constrained her now felt lighter. She had become anchored not in external validation but in internal clarity. She touched the mirror lightly, as though greeting an old friend she had finally come to recognise.

"This is who I am now," she whispered.

Not louder.
Not harder.
Not tougher.
Just clearer.

The Maturity She Embodies, Not Announces

The next morning, she entered a high-stakes meeting. The room was tense, the agenda contentious. A junior diplomat whispered nervously beside her.

"Ambassador… what if this goes wrong?"

She placed a steady hand on his arm.

"Then we respond," she said. "Not react."

He exhaled, visibly calmer.

Her maturity was not something she announced.
It was something she embodied.
It was visible in her eyes, her tone, her decisions, her restraint.

It was the maturity that came from having lived many lives within one career, from having seen the world in all its beauty and brutality, and from having shouldered responsibility that reshaped her.

Ultimately, she understood that the seasons of her diplomatic journey had not merely aged her; they had refined her. They had sculpted her into a woman who led with depth, moved with intention, spoke with clarity, and stood with a steadiness that could not be taught, only lived.

Her maturity was not loud.
It was not dramatic.
It was not performative.
It was quiet.
It was earned.
It was enduring.

And it became one of the most powerful instruments she carried into every room she entered.

Lessons Learnt

She learns that maturity is not a milestone but a quiet evolution, a slow unfolding shaped by seasons rather than by moments. She discovers that steadiness is not the absence of emotion but its mastery, and that clarity grows in silence while discernment deepens with experience. She realises that depth is formed not only in triumph but also in surrender, and that the most enduring maturity is not declared but lived. And she understands that the woman she has become is not the product of age but of awareness.

CHAPTER THIRTY-SEVEN

The Identity Reconstruction After Diplomatic Service

The Soft Unravelling of a Life Once Defined by Urgency

The late afternoon sun hung low over Bern, casting a warm, honey-colored glow across the cobblestones as Ambassador Elena Marković departed from the embassy for the final occasion. The brass plaque affixed to the wall glimmered subtly behind her, reflecting a distinguished career that had spanned continents, crises, and numerous chambers where she had steadfastly upheld her nation's voice.

She halted at the entrance, her hand resting momentarily on the cool metal of the doorframe, as if her body required a pause to synchronise with what her mind had already acknowledged: she would not be returning tomorrow.

The city proceeded around her with its customary quiet elegance. Cyclists moved past with effortless grace. Church bells resonated in the distance, their sound drifting through the air like a gentle reminder that time continued to progress, even as her world seemed to stand still momentarily. The Aare River shimmered beneath the soft light, its surface rippling like a silk ribbon gently stirred by the wind.

For the first time in decades, Elena walked without a destination.
No briefing folder pressed against her palm.
No encrypted phone vibrating with urgency.
No mental rehearsal of diplomatic lines.
No invisible weight of representation is tightening her shoulders.

Her steps were unhurried.
Her breath was unforced.
Her mind was startlingly still.

There comes a moment in the life of a female diplomat when the world's demands begin to loosen their grip, when urgency softens into something gentler, and when the identity she wore like armour begins to unfasten. This transition is not ceremonial. It is not marked by protocol or applause. It unfolds slowly, like dawn spreading across the horizon.

In that gentle shift, she begins to encounter a different version of herself, the woman who emerges after the work.

This woman is not the diplomat recognised in the corridors of power. She is not the strategist, the negotiator, or the representative. She is not the individual burdened with crises or nations on her shoulders. She is the person beneath the titles, the discipline, and the performance. She is the woman she once was and the woman she has become through her work.

A Breath Beyond Duty

On her initial morning of liberty, Elena seated herself beside the Aare River, as the early light cast a gentle glow across the water. She observed the current moving with a composure she had not previously permitted herself to experience. The river did not rush; it did not strain; it merely flowed, steady, confident, and unburdened. She realised she was not anticipating crises, rehearsing statements, or scrutinising her surroundings for diplomatic cues. Instead, she was merely present, completely, wholly, without fragmentation.

A small group of rowers glided past, their oars slicing the water in perfect synchrony. A dog barked in the distance. A child laughed. A tram bell chimed softly as it crossed the bridge.

The world was moving, but not towards her. Not through her. Not demanding anything of her.

For the first time in many years, she felt her nervous system exhale. She felt her body unclench after decades of vigilance. She felt her mind settle into a rhythm not dictated by global events. She placed her hand on her chest, surprised by the softness of her own heartbeat.

In that stillness, she recognised that she was not losing herself.
She was meeting herself again.

Integration, Not Erasure

The reconstruction of identity after diplomatic service is not about erasing previous personas. It is about integrating the experiences and qualities she has accumulated.

Elena recognised that she was no longer defined solely by her actions, but also by the endurance and internalisation of those experiences. She carried the wisdom accrued from years of navigating complex situations. She bore the scars of battles fought in silence. She held the resilience of a life dedicated to service.

But she also preserved the gentleness she had once concealed for self-protection. She rediscovered the softness she had tucked away beneath protocol. She reclaimed the parts of herself she had muted to survive the demands of the role.

She had evolved into a woman who acknowledged her intrinsic worth without relying on institutional validation. She recognised her voice without needing to raise it. She trusted her intuition without awaiting external authorisation. She now understands that identity is not a performance. Identity is a return.

The Return

In the weeks that followed, she learned to rest—not merely the brief pause between crises, but the profound repose of a nervous system no longer in a constant state of alert. She acquired the ability to feel fully, rather than in controlled fragments.

She learned to make choices guided by desire and alignment, rather than obligation. She recognised that the body retains memories the mind attempts to forget, and that healing is not a luxury but a vital reclamation.

She found herself awakening without dread, dining without haste, and strolling without calculation. She gradually began to observe the minor details she had previously overlooked, such as the manner in which sunlight filters through her curtains; the warmth of a cup of tea embraced in her palms; the softness of her laughter when it emerges unexpectedly; the quiet pleasure of unstructured time; and the relief derived from not being needed by the world.

She came to realise that she was not distancing herself from her purpose; rather, she was progressing towards her true self.

The Challenges of Reclaiming Herself

Yet reconstruction was not without its challenges. She had to learn to live without the structure that once anchored her days. She had to learn to live without the urgency that once drove her decisions. She had to learn to live without the institutional identity that once defined her worth. She had to learn to live as herself, not in her role.

There were mornings when she woke to the phantom weight of responsibility pressing on her chest. There were evenings when silence felt too wide, too unfamiliar. There were moments when she wondered who she was without the title, without the mission, without the machinery of diplomacy behind her.

For years, she embodied the woman the world required. Now she had to become the woman she needed to be. She confronted the quiet fear that, without the title, she might disappear. *But she also faced the deeper truth: without the title, she could finally appear.*

The Moment She Realises She Is Free

One morning, seated once again by the river, Elena watched the sunlight shimmer across the water. A gentle breeze brushed her cheek. A leaf drifted past, carried effortlessly on the current. She realised she no longer needed to prove herself to others. She no longer needed to anticipate the next crisis. She no longer needed to bear the burden of representation.

She was free to be a woman with a life, a heart, and a story beyond the apparatus of the state.

In that moment, she understood something profound: **The end of diplomatic service is not the end of identity. It is the beginning of authenticity.**

"Freedom," she thought, "is not the absence of duty. It is the presence of self."

The Woman Who Emerges

The woman who emerges after the work is not a diminished version of the diplomat. She is the distilled, clarified, truest version. Elena reconnected with the parts of herself she had set aside, the hobbies she had abandoned, the friendships she had paused, and the dreams she had postponed. She rediscovered joy in small things: morning light, unhurried meals, laughter unaccompanied by the ring of a phone. She learned to inhabit her own life again, not as an extension of an institution, but as a person in her own right.

She understood that her legacy lay not only in the agreements she negotiated or the crises she managed, but also in the lives she touched, the barriers she broke, and the paths she cleared. She realised that the work shaped her, but it did not fully define her.

Wholeness as Her New Identity

Ultimately, she understood that reconstructing her identity after diplomatic service was not about becoming someone new. It was about becoming whole.
Someone complete.
Someone free.

Because the work had demanded parts of her life, it now asked for all of her.

Lessons Learnt

She realises that identity after service is not a void but a return, a quiet homecoming to the self she once subdued beneath duty. She discovers that the woman beneath the diplomat was never lost; she was only waiting. She understands that wholeness is not found in titles but in presence, not in duty but in authenticity, not in performance but in truth. And she recognises that the conclusion of her diplomatic service is not a termination but an emergence, the beginning of a life lived in its entirety, with depth, softness, and the fullness of her true self.

PART IV

RETURN, LEGACY, AND THE FUTURE OF WOMEN IN DIPLOMACY

"She is the quiet between storms, the space where nations breathe. "- Kemi.

Architectural Prelude

Legacy does not announce itself. It gathers slowly, accumulating in the quiet spaces between decisions, in the weight of responsibilities borne without witness, and in the subtle shifts she leaves behind in the institutions she steadies. It is not loud. It is not ceremonial. It is not the applause that follows a speech or the headline that accompanies a treaty.

Legacy is the architecture she builds in silence, the invisible scaffolding that outlives her presence. It begins in the rooms where she held her composure when others faltered, in the corridors where she softened a culture without ever naming the labour, in the meetings where she widened the path for voices that had long been ignored. It forms in the way she carries herself, in the tone she sets, in the boundaries she defends, in the clarity she embodies. It forms in the way she teaches others, not through instruction, but through example.

Part Four enters the terrain of what endures.
Not the visible achievements.
Not the public victories.
Not the moments captured in photographs.

But the **subtle structures** shaped by her presence, the shifts in institutional behaviour, the recalibration of expectations, the quiet normalisation of women's authority in spaces that once resisted it.

This is where her influence becomes architectural: layered, deliberate, and often unacknowledged.

Here, the female diplomat is no longer defined by the urgency of crises or the demands of representation. She is defined by what remains after she steps out of the room, the culture she has softened, the pathways she has widened, the possibilities she has made imaginable for the women who will follow.

Legacy, for her, is not a destination.
It is a quiet construction.
A slow, deliberate shaping of space.
A structure built in silence, held together by integrity, and carried forward by those who inherit the rooms she once steadied.

This Prelude marks the beginning of a deeper movement, the architecture of what she leaves behind, the imprint of her presence, and the enduring resonance of a life lived with intention.

CHAPTER THIRTY-EIGHT

The Architecture of the Legacy She Builds in Silence

When Legacy Becomes a Quiet Form of Power

Legacy is often imagined as something loud, a monument, a headline, a ceremony, a name engraved in stone. But for the female diplomat, legacy rarely announces itself. It does not arrive with applause or public recognition. It does not demand to be remembered. Instead, it grows quietly, almost imperceptibly, in the spaces where she chooses integrity over convenience, courage over comfort, and truth over institutional expectation.

For her, legacy is not a performance. It is a discipline. It is the slow, deliberate construction of influence in environments never designed to hold her weight. It is the architecture she builds in silence, not because she lacks a voice, but because the institution lacks the capacity to hear her without distortion.

On her final evening in Singapore, Ambassador Sofia Marković stepped onto the balcony of her residence as the sky dissolved into shades of rose and amber. The humidity clung to her skin, carrying the scent of rain that had not yet fallen. Below, the city pulsed with its usual rhythm, efficient, luminous, alive, yet she felt a stillness within herself she had not known in years. It was the stillness of a woman who finally understood the architecture of what she had built.

Legacy, she realised, is not a moment. It is an accumulation. It is the layering of choices made when no one is watching. It is the quiet architecture of influence that grows in the shadows of institutional structures never designed to hold her.

An Architecture of Herself

As dusk deepened, Sofia perceived the culmination of her final assignment not as a burden but as an acknowledgement. Her years of navigating crises, negotiating treaties, and representing her nation with unwavering resolve had culminated in this moment.

Standing on the balcony, she recognised that her legacy extended beyond the speeches she delivered and the documents she signed.

Those were the visible evidence of her service.

The true legacy resided elsewhere. It resided in the young officer who once faltered during a briefing, her voice scarcely audible. Sofia had subsequently invited her into her office, offering reassurance, guidance, and tacit permission to occupy space with confidence. That officer now conducts negotiations with a certainty that inspires confidence in every room she enters.

It resided in the policy reforms Sofia championed, reforms destined to persist beyond her tenure and to influence the institution in ways that would transcend her personal imprint.

It resided in the cultural transformation she catalysed, empowering women to lead without apology, without diminishment, and without feeling compelled to perform gratitude for their presence.

At that moment, she grasped that legacy was not merely the narrative she constructed about herself. Instead, it was the story others would recount long after her departure.

Legacy as Institutional Disruption

Diplomatic institutions rarely acknowledge the silent efforts of women. They commend outcomes rather than the unseen scaffolding that enables them. They extol stability without recognising the emotional labour that sustains it. They commend reforms without acknowledging the behind-the-scenes struggles required to implement them.

Over the years, Sofia had come to understand that institutions often oppose the very changes they profess to support. They advocate inclusion while maintaining hierarchical structures. They celebrate diversity while preserving barriers that mute certain voices. They laud women's resilience while benefiting from the exertion it entails.

Her legacy, therefore, was not merely the achievements she accomplished. It was the institutional complicity she challenged. She confronted the unspoken rules that dictated who could speak, lead, and be visible. She declined to offer unwarranted gratitude for opportunities she had rightfully earned. She asserted that her presence was not symbolic but structural. She created space not only for herself but also for future women.

Legacy, she realised, is not solely what she creates. It is also what she refuses to permit.

The Night She Understood the Cost of Her Legacy

Years before Singapore, there was a night that shaped her understanding of legacy, a night without applause, without witnesses, without the comfort of recognition.

She had just concluded a week of intense negotiations in Geneva. The discussions had been fraught, the stakes high, and the atmosphere tense. She had maintained composure throughout, demonstrating self-sacrifice in her leadership. She had mediated between delegations that refused to make eye contact. She had endured the frustration, anger, and fear, all while preserving the calm expected of her.

When she returned to her hotel room that night, she removed her heels, loosened her hair, and sat on the floor beside the bed. The silence felt weighty, not due to its quietness, but because of its honesty. It revealed the toll of her work—the emotional labour, missed birthdays, strained relationships caused by distance, and the parts of herself she had sidelined to uphold the institution.

She leaned her head against the wall and whispered into the dimness:

"I hope this is building something."

It was not a question. It was a plea.

She did not yet know that the legacy she was building would be measured not by accolades but by the quiet transformations she enabled. She did not yet know that the officers she mentored would carry her influence into rooms she would never enter. She did not yet know that the boundaries she set would become precedents. She did not yet know that the institution would one day shift not because it wanted to, but because she had made it impossible to remain unchanged.

That night, she understood the cost.
Years later, in Singapore, she finally understood the return.

Legacy as Quiet Integrity

Sofia's legacy was not constructed through grand gestures. Instead, it was established through quiet integrity, an attribute that does not seek recognition and persists even when unobserved. She cultivated her legacy by steadfastly upholding her values in environments where compromise would have been more facile. Her legacy was also evident in her respectful treatment of others, even when the institution failed to do so. She maintained her composure even as chaos threatened to engulf the room.

Her legacy resided in the reassurance she provided late at night to a junior officer overwhelmed by responsibility. It was reflected in the handwritten note she left for her successor, imbued with wisdom accumulated over years of service. Furthermore, it manifested in the steadiness she brought to tense negotiations, the clarity that redirected conflicts, and the boundaries she established that ultimately became institutional norms. Such moments seldom attracted headlines; however, they profoundly influenced history.

Legacy as Structural Resistance

To build a legacy in silence is not to accept invisibility. It is to resist the institution's expectation that women must perform their value to be acknowledged. Sofia understood that her legacy was not loud because it did not need to be. It was not tied to her name because it was tied to her influence.

It was not dependent on her presence because it had already taken root in the people she had shaped. Her legacy was a form of structural resistance, a refusal to allow the institution to remain unchanged. It was a quiet rewriting of the rules. It was a recalibration of what leadership looked like. It disrupted the assumption that authority must be loud, masculine, or performative.

Her legacy was not an echo. It was an architecture.

The Legacy That Outlives Her Presence

As the first drops of rain began to fall, Sofia remained on the balcony, letting the coolness settle onto her skin. She realised that the legacy she built in silence was the most profound because it did not depend on her being remembered. It depended on the transformation she had already set in motion.

Her legacy was not the narrative she recounted about herself. It was the narrative others would recount long after her departure. *The truest legacy, she understood, is the one that continues without needing to be named.*

Lessons Learnt

She learns that legacy is not built in moments of visibility but in seasons of consistency. She discovers that influence is not measured by recognition but by transformation. She realises that the most enduring legacies are not loud but lived, carried quietly in the lives of those she touched, in the systems she shifted, and in the courage she inspired. She understands that legacy is not the story she tells about herself but the story others will tell about her. Ultimately, she recognises that the architecture of her legacy is not built on applause but on the silent, steady, unyielding work of becoming the kind of leader whose impact outlasts her presence.

CHAPTER THIRTY-NINE

The Resilience of the Female Diplomat in the Split-Second World

When Time Becomes an Adversary

New York is a city that refuses to slow down. It pulses with a rhythm that feels almost human, urgent, restless, unpredictable, and unapologetically alive. At dawn, the streets are already awake, humming with the low growl of buses and the impatient rhythm of honking taxis. By mid-morning, the pavements become rivers of motion, carrying thousands of people in every direction at once. Wall Street analysts clutch their coffees like survival gear, nannies push prams with the precision of marathon runners, delivery cyclists negotiate with gravity, and tourists spin in circles, overwhelmed by skyscrapers that swallow the sky.

For diplomats, New York is not merely a city; it is a battlefield of time. It is the place where global politics collide with personal responsibilities in real time, where a woman can be drafting a Security Council intervention at 9:03 a.m. and sprinting to catch the E train at 9:07 a.m., where the world's crises and her children's needs share the same calendar, often on the same line.

It is a city that demands simultaneity, the ability to live multiple lives at once without dropping any of them.

For Ms R. Adebayo, senior diplomat and mother of two, New York was not chaos. It was choreography.

It was the split-second world she had mastered.

Scene One: The Day She Carried Two Worlds

At 2:58 p.m., she was seated in Conference Room 7 at the United Nations, attentively listening as delegates debated the final wording of a humanitarian clause. The negotiations had prolonged for hours, and the atmosphere was laden with tension. She discreetly checked her watch. Her children's school in Queens was scheduled to close at 3:30 p.m., and the driver was impeded by traffic. Her spouse was on a work-related trip, and no backup was available.

She leaned toward her deputy and whispered, "Hold the line on paragraph twelve. I will return in an hour."

She gathered her documents, discreetly exited the room, and swiftly proceeded through the United Nations' basement corridor, a passage regularly used by diplomats for unobstructed passage. She successfully passed the security checkpoint, acknowledged the guard with familiarity, and then stepped into the rainy weather.

By 3:27 p.m., she was standing outside the school gate, holding an umbrella in one hand and her phone in the other, responding to a message from her capital requesting her assessment of a new amendment before the 5 p.m. deadline.

Her children ran toward her, their backpacks bouncing and faces bright with joy. She embraced them, ushered them into the vehicle, handed them snacks, and said, "Mommy has to return to work briefly, okay?"

They nodded in understanding; they were accustomed to such routines.

By 4:12 p.m., she had returned to the mission, and the children were settled in the small conference room with colouring books. At the same time, she briefed her capital regarding the evolving dynamics of the negotiations.

By 5:03 p.m., she was back at the UN, stepping into the room just as the chair called for final comments.

No one in the room knew she had crossed boroughs twice in the last two hours.
No one knew she had balanced national interest with maternal duty in the same breath.
No one knew she had carried two worlds on her shoulders without dropping either.

This is the resilience of the female diplomat, lived, not declared.

Resilience as a Form of Intellectual Labour

The world often romanticises resilience, treating it as a personality trait rather than a form of labour. However, for the female diplomat, resilience is not an innate quality; it is constructed and engineered. It results from emotional regulation, cognitive flexibility, and the capacity to shift between identities within seconds.

Her resilience extends beyond mere endurance; it encompasses the ability to transition seamlessly between roles—transforming from mother to negotiator, from caregiver to strategist, and from crisis manager at home to crisis manager at the United Nations. It involves the capacity to hold multiple realities in her mind simultaneously without succumbing to the weight of any of them.

This is not resilience as the world imagines it. This is resilience as **intellectual architecture**. It requires the capacity to compartmentalise without disconnecting; the ability to prioritise without guilt; the discipline to remain composed while her mind is split between continents and classrooms; the emotional intelligence to regulate fear, urgency, and responsibility simultaneously.

Her resilience is not accidental. It is a skill, one that the institution depends on but rarely acknowledges.

When Everything Collided at Once

Two months later, on a cold January morning, another test arrived. At 7:42 a.m., just as she was preparing to leave for a high-level briefing, her youngest child vomited on the living room carpet. At 7:44 a.m., her phone buzzed with a message from the mission: the host country had changed its position, and she was needed immediately. At 7:46 a.m., the school nurse called to say that her older child had a fever and needed to be picked up.

Three emergencies.
Two children.
One diplomat.
Zero margin for error.

She cleaned the carpet, called a neighbour to stay with the younger child, grabbed her coat, and rushed to the school. By 8:19 a.m., she was at the mission, hair slightly damp, breath steady, briefing her team on the implications of the host country's shift. No one knew she had been on her knees scrubbing a carpet less than an hour earlier.

No one knew she had wiped a child's forehead before stepping into a geopolitical storm. No one knew she had already lived a full day before the world even began its own. *This is the resilience of the female diplomat, invisible, instinctive, indispensable.*

Resilience as Structural Resistance

The institution benefits from her resilience while refusing to name the cost. It praises her composure but ignores the emotional labour that sustains it. It applauds her ability to multitask but remains indifferent to the toll it takes. It celebrates her professionalism but overlooks the personal sacrifices that make that professionalism possible.

Her resilience becomes a form of **structural resistance**, a refusal to allow the institution's demands to break her, even when the institution does not protect her. She learns to navigate systems that were not designed for her, to create stability in environments that thrive on urgency, to carry burdens that are invisible to those who depend on her.

Her resilience is not a gift to the institution.
It is a survival strategy within it.

The Night She Saved Two Worlds

One evening in March, she was hosting a reception when her phone vibrated with a message from home: her child had lost their inhaler. Her heart tightened. At the same moment, a colleague whispered that a delegation was threatening to walk out and they needed her immediately.

Two crises.
One personal.
One political.
Both urgent.
Both hers.

She excused herself, stepped into a quiet corner, and called home. She guided her child through slow breathing, instructed the nanny on where to find the spare inhaler, and waited until she heard her child's breath steady.

Then she returned to the reception, shoulders squared, voice calm, and negotiated the delegation back into the room. No one knew she had just prevented a medical emergency. No one knew she had been a mother and a mediator in the same minute. No one knew she had saved two worlds at once. *This is the resilience of the female diplomat, the resilience of simultaneity.*

The Quiet Truth of Her Strength

Her resilience is not loud. It is lived. It is the quiet discipline of a woman who refuses to let either world collapse. She learns to regulate her emotions in split seconds, to shift from fear to composure, from urgency to calm, from personal crisis to diplomatic clarity. She learns to carry multiple realities without losing herself in any of them.

The world sees her speeches, her statements, her negotiations, her composure. But the world will never see the school run between resolutions, the medical emergencies between meetings, the emotional labour between paragraphs, the whispered prayers in the elevator, the exhaustion she hides behind a steady voice. Her resilience is not the absence of struggle. It is the mastery of movement between worlds.

Lessons Learnt

She learns that resilience is not the absence of crisis but the capacity to navigate crises without losing sight of her core self. She discovers that the strength of a female diplomat is not forged in moments of tranquillity but in managing multiple pressing demands simultaneously, the diplomatic, the domestic, the emotional, and the political, all requiring her immediate attention. She realises that her resilience is not a performance for external approval but a private discipline, a subtle mastery of transitions that remains unacknowledged yet essential.

She understands that the institution benefits from her ability to uphold two worlds without acknowledging the attendant costs. She recognises that her resilience is not incidental but deliberately constructed, cultivated through repetition, necessity, and the emotional labour she performs in silence. She learns that her strength lies not in prioritising one world over another, but in refusing to abandon either.

Ultimately, she understands that the resilience of the female diplomat is neither loud nor theatrical nor publicly celebrated.

It is experienced in the split seconds when she manages to preserve both worlds without ever drawing notice.

CHAPTER FORTY

The Strategic Discipline of Staying the Course

When Pressure Comes from Every Direction

The female diplomat occupies a pivotal position at the intersection of global expectations and internal political dynamics, bearing the burden of her country's reputation while navigating the quiet tumult within her own delegation. The international community observes the flags, the speeches, and the formal declarations. It does not perceive the moments when she is confined by forces on both sides, adversaries across the table, and betrayal behind her.

On a humid afternoon in Geneva, Ambassador Liana Moretti found herself in precisely such a situation. The atmosphere inside the Palais des Nations was heavy, thick with tension from stalled negotiations. Delegates shuffled papers with the impatience of those who had been in the same room for too long. The fluorescent lights hummed overhead, casting a sterile glow over faces that had grown weary from the rigours of geopolitics.

Her country was under considerable pressure over a regional security agreement. Influential states were advocating concessions that would diminish her nation's strategic standing. Simultaneously, her own capital had begun to waver, dispatching mixed instructions that contradicted the mandate she had diligently defended for months.

She perceived the shift before it was articulated.

Emails became vague.
Calls went unanswered.
A colleague in her delegation avoided her eyes during a briefing.
A senior advisor suddenly became "unavailable."

Something was moving beneath the surface, and she was expected to stand firm while the ground shifted under her feet.

She straightened her notes, lifted her chin, and prepared to defend a position she was no longer sure her capital still supported.

The Betrayal Behind the Flag

The betrayal arrived quietly, as it often does. During a closed-door session, she presented her country's long-held position with clarity and conviction. Her voice was steady, her arguments precise, her posture unshakeable. She had done this work long enough to command a room without raising her voice. Moments later, the chair cleared his throat and announced that her capital had communicated a revised stance, one she had never seen, one that undermined everything she had just defended.

A murmur rippled through the room.
Delegations exchanged glances.
Someone scribbled a note.
Someone else smirked.

Her credibility was punctured in real time. She felt the heat rise in her chest, but her face remained composed. She asked for a brief suspension, stepped out of the room, and dialled her ministry.

No answer.

She tried her deputy.

Silence.

She tried the political director.

Voicemail.

Only then did she understand: the decision had been made without her, leaving her to absorb the impact alone. When she returned to the room, a colleague from her delegation leaned in and whispered, "They didn't want to tell you. They thought you'd resist." It was not only the ministry that had shifted. Someone on her team had known and chosen not to warn her. She had been strategically isolated, not by adversaries, but by those who should have stood beside her.

Yet she did not retreat. She did not crumble. She refused to let the humiliation dictate her next move. She inhaled slowly, straightened her back, and continued the negotiation with the same precision she had shown from the beginning. Her dignity became her shield.

The Night She Rebuilt Herself

That evening, long after the building had emptied, she sat alone in her office overlooking Lake Geneva. The city lights shimmered on the water, casting long reflections that trembled in the breeze. She removed her heels, rested her feet flat on the floor, and let the silence settle around her. She replayed the moment of betrayal in her mind, the announcement, the glances, the sudden shift in the room's temperature. She felt the sting, the sharpness of being blindsided, the ache of being left unprotected by the very institution she served.

But beneath the hurt, something else stirred, a clarity she had earned through years of weathering diplomatic storms. “They may have moved the line,” she whispered to herself, “but I will not lose the horizon.” She opened her laptop and began drafting a new strategy that aligned with the revised mandate while still protecting her country’s core interests. She worked through the night, her fingers moving with the discipline of someone who had rebuilt herself before. By dawn, she had a plan. Not because her capital supported her. Not because her delegation stood with her. But because she refused to let betrayal define the outcome.

Holding the Line When the Line Moves

The days that followed were a test of endurance and clarity. External pressure intensified.

Allies questioned her reliability.
Opponents sensed weakness.
Journalists speculated about fractures within her delegation.

And still, her capital remained silent, not explaining the sudden shift, no guidance for the path ahead. However, Liana understood a crucial lesson that only experienced diplomats learn: maintaining the course does not mean clinging to a rigid stance. It signifies adhering to the underlying purpose beneath the stance. It involves navigating challenges without losing sight of the overarching goal. It entails adapting without yielding. It requires flexibility without compromise. She recalibrated her strategy accordingly. She also rebuilt trust with sceptical delegations through discreet, late-night dialogues in dimly lit corridors.

She reframed her country's revised stance to preserve its core interests. She confronted the colleague who had withheld information, not with anger, but with a calm that unsettled him more than any outburst could. And she continued to show up, meeting after meeting, session after session, even when the institution that sent her had left her exposed.

Her strength lay not in the loudness of her resistance, but in the steadiness of her presence. She refused to be erased by the betrayal. She refused to be defined by the moment she was undermined. She refused to abandon the work simply because others had abandoned her.

The Triumph Hidden in Her Endurance

Months later, when the agreement was finalised, the world hailed it as a diplomatic breakthrough. Cameras flashed. Statements were issued. Commentators praised the "remarkable resilience" of her delegation. But no one knew the truth behind the triumph.

No one knew how close the process had come to collapse.
No one knew how many nights she had spent alone, drafting new language to salvage what others had compromised.
No one knew how many times she had been tempted to walk away, not from the negotiation, but from the institution that had betrayed her.

Her triumph was not in the signing ceremony. Her triumph was in the moments she chose to stay, despite every reason to leave.
Her triumph was in the clarity she maintained when others blurred the lines.

Her triumph was in the discipline to remain steady in a landscape designed to shake her.

She understands that diplomacy is not only the art of negotiation; it is the art of endurance.

It is the ability to hold fast to a vision amid uncertainty, to withstand pressure without breaking, and to continue the work even when the institution itself becomes the obstacle.

The world remembers the agreements she signs. But the true victory lies in the resilience that makes those agreements possible.

Lessons Learnt

She learns that staying the course is not an act of stubbornness but a strategic move. She discovers that endurance is not passive but profoundly powerful. She realises that progress is often invisible until it becomes undeniable. And she understands that her greatest victories are not the ones celebrated publicly, but the ones sustained quietly through discipline, clarity, and unwavering resolve, even when betrayal comes from within.

CHAPTER FORTY-ONE

The Authority of Her Convictions in Diplomatic Space

The Quiet Power of a Woman Who Knows What She Believes

The morning light filtered through the tall windows of the Palais des Nations in Geneva, casting long, deliberate shadows across the marble floor. The building carried the weight of decades, treaties signed, crises debated, promises made and broken. It was a place where words shaped destinies, where silence could be as consequential as speech, and where truth often bent under political pressure. Yet as Deputy Permanent Representative Laila Men Sallam walked along the corridor towards Conference Room XVII, a steady calm settled into her bones.

Her influence was not loud. It was not theatrical. It did not demand attention. It was the quiet authority of a woman who knew what she believed, deeply, intimately, irrevocably. Her convictions were not slogans crafted for applause. They were not borrowed beliefs inherited from institutions. They were the distilled essence of her lived experience, shaped by the desert winds of Nouakchott, her grandmother's stories, her community's resilience, and the lessons carved into her by years spent navigating diplomatic spaces where truth was negotiable and pressure persistent.

She had learned early that conviction was not noise. It was clarity. And clarity, when held with dignity, could shift the atmosphere of a room more powerfully than volume ever could.

The Moment She Refused to Yield

The morning's negotiation was expected to be routine, a review of a draft resolution addressing regional security concerns. But as Laila read the text projected on the screen, her breath tightened. The language was elegant, polished, and dangerously incomplete. It flattened complexity into simplicity, erased nuance, and reduced lived realities to diplomatic abstractions. In doing so, it risked misrepresenting the very people the resolution claimed to protect.

She leaned forward, her eyes scanning the clauses again. A seemingly harmless phrase carried implications that could shift responsibility away from those who held power and place an undue burden on communities already stretched thin. She knew what this meant. She had seen the consequences of such language before: misinterpretation, misallocation of resources, and narratives that distorted the truth.

Before the meeting began, a colleague leaned in and whispered, "Don't push too hard today. They want consensus. Just let it pass." Another added, "Flexibility is important. We can adjust later." A third, more senior diplomat, offered a gentle warning: "Don't isolate yourself. The room is tired. They want agreement, not debate."

But Laila felt the weight of the moment settle in her chest. She knew the details were not mere technicalities. They represented lives, sovereignty, and dignity. She knew silence would be easier, more convenient, and more politically palatable. But she also knew that silence would be a betrayal—not only of her role, but of her truth.

When the Chair opened the floor for comments, she raised her hand. When she spoke, her voice was steady. Not loud. Not forceful. But unmistakably clear.

"Mr Chair, with respect, the language in paragraph six does not reflect the realities on the ground. It risks mischaracterising the situation and may lead to unintended consequences for the communities most affected."

A ripple moved through the room. Delegates shifted in their seats. Some frowned. Some looked down at their papers. Some exchanged glances that said, Why now? Why her? Why this?

But Laila continued, her tone unwavering. She did not speak to impress. She spoke to illuminate. She spoke because she could not do otherwise.

Gradually, the atmosphere shifted, not because she overwhelmed the room, but because she refused to yield to what she knew was wrong. Her authority came not from rank, but from alignment between her beliefs and her expression. It was the authority of a woman who had learned that truth, when spoken with integrity, had its own gravitational pull.

The Authority That Does Not Need Volume

There is a particular kind of authority that does not need volume. It does not need theatrics. It does not need dominance. It is the authority of a woman who stands firmly by her convictions, even when the room prefers her silence.

Laila embodied that authority.

Her convictions were rooted in the stories her grandmother told her, stories of endurance, justice, and the quiet strength of women who held families and communities together without recognition. They were rooted in the resilience of her people, who had learned to survive in landscapes both physical and political.

They were rooted in the lessons of past failures, the scars of missteps, and the hopes of future generations who deserved better.

Her authority was not stubbornness. It was in alignment with the truth. It was the clarity that comes from knowing that integrity is not negotiable, even when everything else is.

The Conviction That Clarifies Compromise

Diplomacy is often described as the art of negotiation through compromise. However, Laila understood that compromise devoid of conviction amounts to surrender. Her duty was not to reject compromise outright, but to distinguish between strategic concessions and those that were detrimental. She observed the consequences of diplomats conceding too hastily: distorted narratives, misrepresented communities, and policies that diverged from reality.

Conversely, she recognised the consequences when diplomats refused to compromise at all: stalemates, resentment, and lost opportunities for progress. Her authority lay in her ability to navigate the tension between these two extremes. Her convictions informed her compromises, enabling her to distinguish between adjustments that could be made and essential protections.

They provided stability when the environment grew hostile, centred her amid mounting pressure, and preserved her integrity when convenience was prioritised over truth.

After the meeting, a young diplomat approached her quietly. “I didn’t agree with everything you said,” he admitted, “but I respected how you said it. You made us think. You made us reconsider.”

That was influence.

Not dominance.

Not victory. Influence.

Later, a senior ambassador pulled her aside. “You were right to raise the issue,” he said. “We needed that clarity. Thank you for not letting it pass.” That was legacy. Not applause. Not recognition. Legacy.

In the end, she realised that her greatest influence did not come from speaking the loudest, but from standing firmest. The world did not always agree with her, yet it always felt the weight of a woman who knew exactly what she believed.

Lessons Learnt

She learns that conviction is not rigidity but clarity. She discovers that authority is not about volume but about alignment. She realises that influence is not force but integrity. And she understands that the diplomat who stands firmly in her truth reshapes the room simply by refusing to abandon what she knows is right.

CHAPTER FORTY-TWO

The Quiet Authority of Solitary Leadership

The Leader That Stands Alone

The winter sun hung low over Vienna, casting a pale gold sheen across the Danube as Ambassador Thandiwe Mbeki walked towards the conference centre. The air was crisp, almost sharp, carrying the faint scent of roasted chestnuts from a nearby vendor. The city moved with its usual elegance, trams gliding along their tracks, pedestrians wrapped in scarves, diplomats hurrying to meetings that would shape policies, alliances, and futures.

Thandiwe walked with a calm that belied the storm gathering within her. She had learned early in her career that leadership did not always require collective action. Sometimes leadership was solitude. It was the quiet authority of standing independently within a sphere of influence, an environment where alliances shifted like sand, where silence became strategy, where every word was weighed, and where the consequences of speech were significant.

Standing alone was not rebellion.
It was not a theatre.
It was not vanity.
It was clarity, the clarity of knowing what must be said even when others hesitated, what must be protected even when others were willing to concede, and who she must be even when the room preferred her silence.

She had not always possessed this clarity. It had been forged through years of watching decisions made in rooms where truth was diluted for convenience, where pressure disguised itself as diplomacy, where silence was rewarded more than courage. She had learned that leadership was not the absence of fear, but the refusal to let fear dictate her voice.

The Lonely Moment

The ministerial meeting scheduled for that morning was expected to be straightforward, primarily a review of a multilateral cooperation framework. However, as the draft text was projected onto the screen, Thandiwe felt her breath tighten. Λ single clause, subtle and technical, yet nearly indiscernible to the untrained eye, carried implications that could jeopardise her region. The phrase appeared innocuous and even progressive, yet she saw its shadow clearly.

She watched sovereignty erode in a single sentence.
She recognised an imbalance masked as cooperation.

She sensed danger lurking in silence.

Around her, delegates nodded, some out of fatigue, others under pressure, and some for convenience. The Chair moved with dispatch, eager to conclude proceedings. The room was gravitating towards consensus, smooth on the surface yet harbouring fissures beneath.

Thandiwe felt the weight of the moment settle in her chest. She knew her intervention could disrupt the room. She knew dissent could isolate her. She knew standing alone could make her memorable in ways not always favourable. She knew some would interpret her stance as obstinacy, others as unnecessary tension, and a few as a political inconvenience.

But she also knew that silence would cost her nation.

She raised her hand.

The Chair hesitated, just for a moment, before acknowledging her. "South Africa, you have the floor."

Thandiwe inhaled slowly, grounding herself in her mother's voice, the one that had carried her through childhood: If you speak, speak the truth. If you stand, stand firm. If you lead, lead with honour.

She began to speak.

Her voice was firm, her arguments precise, her conviction unmistakable. She did not raise her tone. She did not dramatise. She did not apologise. She articulated the truth with a clarity that cut through the room like a blade of light.

Some delegates looked away.
Some frowned.
Some listened more intently than they wished.

The Chair shifted in his seat. A few whispered to their aides. One delegate tapped his pen nervously on his folder. The atmosphere shifted—not dramatically, but undeniably. The room had been drifting towards an easy agreement. Now it was awake. Thandiwe continued, her voice steady. She explained the clause's implications, historical context, regional sensitivities, and potential consequences. She spoke not to win, but to illuminate. She spoke not to dominate, but to anchor the truth. When she finished, the room was silent.

Not hostile.
Not dismissive.
Just silent.

The kind of silence that follows truth spoken without fear.

The Courage to Anchor the Truth

Standing alone is not about winning the room. It is about anchoring the truth. It entails refusing to let pressure distort principles, to let convenience overshadow justice, or to silence what must be said out of fear. Thandiwe had learned that diplomacy was more than the art of agreement; it encompassed the courage to dissent when consensus posed dangers. She recognised that leadership was not invariably a collective endeavour; at times, it was solitary. She understood that the toll of silence often exceeded that of dissent.

After her intervention, the Chair cleared his throat. “Perhaps we should revisit the language,” he said, his tone measured.

A few delegates nodded reluctantly. Others took notes. The clause was reopened, and the conversation shifted.

The room recalibrated.

Thandiwe did not smile or celebrate. She quietly exhaled, aware that she had fulfilled her necessary role.

The Rooms That Shape Her

Some rooms shape a diplomat, rooms where she discovers her courage, understands the demands of leadership, and becomes the woman the world recognises, not because she blends into the room, but because she dares to stand apart.

For Thandiwe, this was one of those rooms.

She remembered the early years of her career, when she had watched senior diplomats navigate similar moments. She remembered those who spoke the truth, even when it was inconvenient. She remembered those who stayed silent and later regretted it. She remembered those who compromised too quickly and those who refused to compromise at all.

She had learned from them all.

She had learned that leadership was not a performance. It was presence.
She had learned that authority was not dominance. It was integrity.
She had learned that courage was not loud. It was steady.
She had learned that standing alone was not isolation. It was a duty.

The Private Fracture Behind the Public Composure

After the meeting, Thandiwe returned to her hotel room overlooking the river. She took off her jacket, set her folder on the desk, and sat on the edge of the bed. The adrenaline that had carried her through the meeting began to fade, leaving a quiet tremor in her hands.

She was not afraid.
She was not uncertain.
She was simply human.

Leadership carried a cost.
Solitary leadership carried a heavier burden.

She closed her eyes and allowed herself a moment of vulnerability, one she could not afford in the meeting room. She felt the weight of responsibility settle on her shoulders, the emotional labour of standing alone, and the quiet ache of knowing that courage often came with solitude.

But she also felt something else, something deeper, steadier, more enduring.

She felt alignment.
She felt integrity.
She felt the truth.

And truth, she knew, was worth the solitude.

The Reflection That Follows Courage

Later that evening, she walked along the riverbank, the city lights shimmering on the water. She thought about the meeting, the clause, and the silence that followed her intervention. She thought about the young diplomats who had watched her, those who would one day face similar moments. She realised solitary leadership was not a burden. It was a calling.

It was the quiet authority of a woman who knew her voice mattered, even when it was the only one speaking.

It was the dignity of a woman who refused to let fear dictate her choices. It was the strength of a woman who knew that once spoken, the truth could not be unsaid.

The Authority of a Woman Who Stands in Truth

In the end, Thandiwe understood that the authority of solitary leadership did not stem from the room's approval. It stemmed from her alignment with what she knew to be right. It stemmed from the courage to speak when silence was easier. It stemmed from the integrity to stand alone when others preferred comfort to clarity.

She knew the world might not always agree with her.

But the world would always feel the weight of her truth.

Lessons Learnt

She learns that solitary leadership is not loneliness but clarity. She discovers that dissent is not disruption but protection. She realises that standing alone is not defiance but duty. And she understands that the authority of a woman who stands in truth can shift the course of a room, a negotiation, and, at times, even history.

CHAPTER FORTY-THREE

The Return to Self: A Diplomatic Homecoming

The Silence That Reveals Her

The aircraft descended gradually over Abuja, its wings penetrating the gentle haze of the late afternoon. From her window seat, Ambassador Bassirat Okon observed the familiar landscape unfold beneath her, red earth, winding roads, clusters of rooftops glinting in the sunlight. This was a view she had witnessed many times; yet today, it appeared different. Today, it resembled a mirror.

There exists a moment in the career of a female diplomat when the surroundings become silent. This silence is not attributable to external factors but rather to an internal transformation. The sounds that previously characterised her days, such as urgency, crises, negotiations, and expectations, gradually receded into the background.

This silence is not emptiness; it is enlightenment.

It is within this tranquillity that she finally perceives something long unheard: her own self.

The resurgence of self is neither theatrical nor ceremonial; it arrives quietly, without fanfare. It manifests in the intervals between duties, in pauses once hurried through, in breaths previously neglected. For many years, she served a cause greater than herself. She bore a nation, carried expectations, shouldered the weight of representation, and undertook the emotional labour of rooms that demanded more than they reciprocated.

However, now, as the wheels touched the runway with a soft thud, she sensed that something had shifted.

She was beginning to carry herself again.

The Homecoming That Begins Within

Her driver met her at the airport, greeting her with a warmth that felt both familiar and foreign. As they drove through the city, Bassirat watched the world move around her, street vendors hawking their wares, children weaving between cars, the hum of life unfolding without urgency. She realised she had spent years in places where she was always slightly outside the rhythm, always adjusting, always performing. Here, she did not need to perform.

When she arrived at her family home, the gate swung open slowly, revealing the compound she had known since childhood. The mango tree still stood tall in the corner, its branches heavy with fruit. The veranda still held the same wooden chairs her father used to sit in in the evenings—the air smelt of earth after rain, of home, of memory.

As she stepped out of the car, she felt the ground beneath her feet as she had not in years. She walked through the courtyard with the quiet awareness of someone who had lived many lives across many landscapes.

She felt sunlight differently.

She heard children's laughter differently. She breathed differently.

She realised she had spent years being outwardly focused and was now rediscovering an inward focus.

The Diplomatic Life: The Return

That night, as she unpacked her suitcase, she found a folder tucked between her clothes, a briefing document from her final week in service.

She sat on the edge of her bed and opened it, scanning the familiar lines of diplomatic language: “urgent,” “immediate action required,” “high-level consultation,” “sensitive matter.”

She remembered the meeting that had produced it. It had taken place in a cold conference room in Brussels, where she had sat across from delegates debating a humanitarian crisis unfolding thousands of miles away. The room had been tense, the stakes high, the pressure immense. She had spoken with precision, her voice steady even as her heart raced. She had advocated fiercely, negotiated tirelessly, and held her ground when others wavered.

But she also remembered the moment afterwards, when she had stepped into the hallway, leaned against the wall, and felt her body tremble. Not from fear. Not from uncertainty. But from exhaustion.

The kind of exhaustion that accumulates quietly over years, settling into the bones, the breath, the soul.

She closed the folder gently and placed it in a drawer.
She was not that woman anymore.
Or rather, she was no longer only that woman.

The Reconnection

The next morning, she woke to the sound of birdsong drifting through her window. For the first time in years, she did not reach for her phone. She did not check her emails. She did not scan headlines. She lay there, listening to the world without urgency.

Her reintegration with herself was not withdrawal from the world; it was a reconnection with the parts of her identity that diplomacy had required her to set aside. She reunited with the woman who cherished silence before it became a strategy, with the woman who loved reading before it became a briefing, with the woman who loved travel before it became a responsibility, and with the woman who loved people before they became delegations.

She reconnected with her softer qualities, her deferred dreams, her neglected body, and her silenced soul.

Later that day, she visited her childhood friend, Adaora, who embraced her with the kind of affection that needed no explanation. They sat under the mango tree, sipping zobo and talking about everything and nothing.

For the first time in years, Laila laughed without calculating the optics of her laughter. She spoke without measuring her words. She existed without performing. It felt like breathing after holding her breath for too long.

The Sacred Journey Back to Herself

The return to one's true self is not selfish; it is sacred. It is the recognition that she cannot spend the rest of her life merely fulfilling a role. She must live as a woman, one who has seen the world from its innermost chambers, borne the weight of decisions shaping nations, stood solitary in rooms of power and emerged with her integrity intact, and endured the emotional storms of diplomacy without losing her humanity.

One evening, she sat alone on the veranda, watching the sky shift from gold to indigo. A stillness settled over her, one she had not felt in decades. She realised she had spent so many years being "Ambassador Okon" that she had forgotten what it felt like simply to be Laila.

She whispered her own name into the night air, as if reintroducing herself.

The Private Fracture That Preceded Her Return

There had been a moment, months before her return, when she realised she could no longer carry on as she had. It had happened in a hotel room in Geneva, after a particularly gruelling negotiation. She had closed the door behind her, taken off her shoes, and sat on the floor, her back against the bed.

She had felt the weight of everything she had carried, the expectations, the crises, the emotional labour, the constant vigilance. She had felt the ache of loneliness that came from being surrounded by people yet unseen. She had felt the quiet grief of a woman who had given so much of herself that she no longer knew where the role ended, and she began.

She had cried, not loudly, not dramatically, but with the soft, steady tears of someone who had reached her limit. In that moment, she had made a promise to herself: When this assignment ends, I will return to myself.

Fully. Completely.

Without apology.

That promise had carried her through the final months of her service.

Now, sitting under the Nigerian sky, she felt that promise fulfilled.

The Life She Once Paused

She returned to the life she had once paused, deferred, and quietly safeguarded in the corners of her heart. She returned to mornings unmarred by urgency, to conversations free of strategy, to relationships free of performance, to joy untainted by guilt.

She returned to cooking with her mother, to reading novels on the veranda, to walking barefoot on the cool tiles of her childhood home. She returned to the softness she had once set aside, the dreams she had once postponed, the woman she had once muted.

She reclaimed the woman she was before the world's demands, and the woman she became in response to them.

The Freedom That Awaits Her

The journey back to herself was not the conclusion of her story; it was the beginning of her freedom. The world had shaped her, but it had not defined her. Diplomacy had stretched her, but it had not consumed her. It demanded parts of her, but it did not take her in her entirety.

She returned to herself because she was now able.
She returned because she must.
She returned because her journey had culminated.

In this return lay the enduring truth:
She was never lost.
She was becoming.

Lesson Learnt

She learns that returning to herself is not retreat but restoration. She discovers that identity is not lost in service, only quietened. She realises that homecoming is not a place but a presence. And she understands that the woman she becomes after diplomacy is not a remnant of her former self but the fullest expression of who she has always been.

PART V

THE PHILOSOPHY OF HER LEADERSHIP

"Her courage is quiet, but it steadies the rooms where nations breathe." – Kemi.

Architectural Prelude

The Philosophy of Her Leadership

At its highest expression, leadership is no longer defined by positional authority, titles, or visibility. It is not the applause after a speech, nor the prestige of a diplomatic posting, nor the weight of a flag behind her. True leadership is the quiet, internal evolution of a woman who has lived long enough within the world's demands to understand her own essence finally.

By the time a female diplomat reaches this stage of her journey, she has already borne the burden of societal expectations to be competent but not intimidating, assertive but not abrasive, visible but not overly conspicuous. She has navigated the solitude inherent in her profession, where decisions are made in isolation and strength is often demonstrated without witnesses. She has managed diplomacy not only across borders but also within her own family, balancing duty with longing, presence with absence, ambition with sacrifice.

She has endured unspoken conventions, mastered the choreography of rooms where she was never meant to lead, and engaged in silent negotiations that have cultivated her inner resilience. She has faced repeated challenges, some public, many invisible, each one refining her into a woman who may be difficult for others to define, yet whom she recognises instinctively.

Part V does not focus on the obstacles she encounters. It concentrates on the woman she becomes.

This is the juncture at which leadership transitions from performance to presence, from reaction to intention, from endurance to authorship.

It is the moment when she no longer evaluates herself through the lens of external pressure but through the clarity of her internal alignment. Here, leadership takes the form of an internal architecture, a framework built on sovereignty, self-governance, and the discipline of knowing who she is when no one is watching. It becomes a practice of alignment, a doctrine of inner authority, a quiet mastery that does not require self-assertion.

These chapters are not about survival.
They are about mastery.
They are not about proving oneself. They are about defining oneself. They are not about navigating the world.
They are about shaping it.

Part V marks the moment when the female diplomat steps into her full stature, not because the world finally recognises her, but because she finally recognises herself. This is the woman who emerges when the fire no longer consumes her but illuminates her. She leads not from fear but from the centre. Not from expectation but from conviction. Not from scarcity but from sovereignty.

This is the woman the world encounters in Part V, the woman she has always been becoming.

CHAPTER FORTY-FOUR

The Philosophy of Her Leadership

The Dawn That Reveals Her

The first light of morning crept across the Muscat coastline, brushing the horizon with soft strokes of rose and amber. Ambassador Hana Al-Khalili stood by her window, watching the sea breathe in slow, deliberate waves. The world was quiet, suspended in the stillness that precedes awakening. In this hour, before the emails, the calls, and the demands of the day, she felt closest to herself.

She had returned from her final diplomatic posting only weeks earlier, yet the rhythm of her life had already shifted. The urgency that once defined her days had softened. The noise that once filled her mind had receded. And in the quiet, she felt something she had not felt in years: the emergence of understanding.

There comes a moment in a diplomat's life when experience ceases to be a mere collection of events and becomes a lens, a way of seeing, discerning, and interpreting the world. For Hana, this moment arrived not in a negotiation room, nor in the aftermath of a crisis, but in the stillness of dawn, when the world was quiet enough for her to hear the truth she had carried all along.

This chapter of her life was not about what she had done. It was about how she had become.

The Moment Her Experience Becomes Understanding

Hana had spent decades navigating the intricate corridors of diplomacy, the negotiations, the silences, the compromises, the crises. She had stood in rooms where truth was diluted for convenience, where power was disguised as cooperation, where silence was rewarded more than courage.

She had learned to read the room, the subtext, the unspoken tensions that shaped outcomes more than words ever could. But now, standing in the quiet of her home, she realised that her leadership had matured into something deeper than skill. It had become a philosophy, a coherent internal logic that guided her actions, her decisions, her presence.

Her leadership was no longer reactive.
It was no longer shaped by circumstance.
It was no longer defined by expectation.

It had become a consciousness.
Not a strategy, a discipline.
Not a posture, a truth she had learned to inhabit.

The Inner Logic That Governs Her Leadership

As she moved through her home that morning, preparing tea with the slow, deliberate movements of someone who had reclaimed her time, Hana reflected on the principles that had shaped her leadership. They were not written down. They were not taught in any academy. They were earned through failure, resilience, revelation, and the quiet courage to choose integrity when convenience beckoned.

She had learned to maintain coherence within systems that rewarded fragmentation. She had learned to uphold principles in environments where everything was negotiable. She had learned to preserve her humanity in spaces that often forgot their own.

Her philosophy was not a doctrine.
It was not a theory.
It was the distilled essence of a life lived in service, reflection, and truth.

Leadership as Evolution, Not Inheritance

Hana had not inherited leadership. She had evolved into it, slowly, painfully, beautifully. Her leadership was shaped by alignment, rupture, recalibration, and truth-telling. It was formed not by the titles she acquired, but by the inner order she learned to protect.

She remembered her early years in service, the uncertainty, the desire to please, the fear of missteps. She remembered the moments when she had compromised too quickly, spoken too softly, or allowed others to define her boundaries. She remembered the nights she lay awake, questioning her decisions, her voice, and her place. But she also remembered the turning points, the moments when she chose clarity over comfort, truth over approval, and integrity over convenience. Those moments had shaped her more than any training, title, or accolade.

Over time, she discovered that leadership was less about authority and more about coherence: the alignment of what she knew, what she believed, and what she was willing to stand for, whether the world was watching or not.

Her leadership was defined not by the volume of her voice but by the integrity of her presence. She led not by demanding space but by embodying clarity. She recognised that influence was not merely the capacity to compel others but the ability to maintain inner order amid competing pressures.

Her leadership was not reactive; it was rooted and resilient in the face of external noise.

Leadership as Discernment, Not Perfection

Over time, Hana learned that leadership was not the pursuit of perfection but the discipline of discernment. It was the ability to distinguish urgency from importance, noise from truth, and movement from progress.

She learned to hold complexity without collapsing into confusion. She learned to hold responsibility without surrendering her humanity. She learned to hold power without losing her centre.

She understood that diplomacy was not merely the management of interests; it was the stewardship of consequences. Every decision sent out a ripple. Every silence carried a cost. Every compromise casts a shadow.

She led with the awareness that her choices transcended the moment, the room, and herself.

Leadership as Courage, Not Certainty

Hana recognised that leadership was not the absence of fear, but its mastery. It was the capacity to act with clarity even when certainty was impossible. It was the willingness to articulate a position when silence would be easier, to pause when momentum was seductive, and to stand alone when consensus became perilous. Her leadership was defined not by the number of followers she had, but by her fidelity to her own truth. She remembered a moment years earlier, when she had been the sole dissenting voice in a room full of agreement.

She had felt the weight of eyes on her, the pressure to conform, the temptation to remain silent. But she had spoken anyway. Not loudly. Not definitely. But clearly.

That moment had taught her that courage was not dramatic.
It was deliberate.
It was quiet.
It was necessary.

Leadership as Practice, Not Performance

She discovered that leadership was not a posture but a practice, cultivated in the quiet hours when no one was watching, in the decisions that never made headlines, and in the integrity she upheld when the world offered easier paths. Her leadership was strengthened by the failures she survived, the disappointments she absorbed, and the resilience she rebuilt in private.

Her leadership was not transactional.
It was transformational.
It did not seek to impress; it sought to illuminate.
It did not aim to dominate; it aimed to elevate.
It did not seek to win; it sought to align the world, however imperfectly, with a deeper sense of justice and possibility.

And in the end, Hana understood that the philosophy of her leadership was simple: To remain whole in a world that asks her to fragment.
To stay clear in a world that rewards ambiguity.
To remain principled in a world that negotiates everything.
To stay human in a world that forgets its own humanity.

This was the leadership she offered.
This was the leadership she embodied.
This was the leadership that endured.

Lessons Learnt

She learns that leadership is not inherited but evolved. She discovers that clarity is more powerful than certainty. She realises that integrity is the foundation of influence. And she understands that her leadership philosophy is not something she performs; it is something she becomes.

CHAPTER FORTY-FIVE

The Weight of the Flag: Identity Meets Institution

The Early Architecture of a Diplomatic Mind

Leadership rarely begins where it is later recognised. It begins quietly, in the unobserved corners of a life, long before titles, postings, or diplomatic credentials enter the picture. Every female diplomat enters the foreign service carrying two parallel histories: the personal formation that shaped her long before she joined, and the institutional architecture she must learn to navigate once she is in. For Amb. (Prof) Olufolake Abdulrasaq, these two histories converged early in her career, revealing that the making of a diplomat is never solely the product of training, rank, or formal instruction. It is the intersection of lived experience and institutional expectation, of early responsibility and bureaucratic scrutiny, and of personal resilience and systemic design.

The institution she entered was not neutral. Like all foreign service bureaucracies, it was structured by hierarchy, ritual, and deeply embedded assumptions about who is expected to lead and who to follow. The female diplomat is often introduced to this system not through hostility but through observation. The institution watches her before it welcomes her. It measures her composure, clarity, ability to interpret silence, and capacity to hold authority in rooms where legitimacy is often gendered.

For Olufolake, who would one day stand before an international assembly and speak for her nation, the earliest leadership lessons were not taught in a training academy. They were learned on the front porch of her childhood home, in the rhythms of responsibility that shaped her long before she grasped their significance. As the first child, she learned early that responsibility is not an abstract concept. It is a lived experience. It is the instinct to anticipate needs before they are voiced. It is the discipline to remain composed when others falter. It is the emotional intelligence to mediate conflict, ease tension, and hold a family together through seasons of uncertainty.

These were not tasks assigned to her; they were expectations woven into the fabric of her upbringing. She learned to read people, sense shifts in mood, intervene with tact, and carry burdens without announcing them. Years later, she would understand that these early experiences were not merely familial duties. They were the foundation of diplomatic leadership. They taught her to listen deeply, observe quietly, respond with clarity, and lead without spectacle. They taught her that authority is not always loud; sometimes it is the quiet steadiness others instinctively trust. They taught her that leadership is not a performance but a posture.

This early training became the invisible scaffolding that sustained her throughout her career. It prepared her for moments she did not anticipate, moments that would test her composure, courage, and capacity to rise without warning. It prepared her for the day when leadership would choose her before she chose it.

A System That Tests Before It Trusts

The institution's first assessment of Olufolake did not take place in a foreign capital. It occurred much earlier, in the unspoken responsibilities of her upbringing. But its first formal test came during a field assignment in Nigeria, a moment that revealed how foreign service bureaucracies often assess women by disruption rather than by preparation.

After completing a foreign service course, officers were assigned to field posts across the country. That year, the ministry had recently recruited several senior officers, who were integrated into the system. Despite being younger and junior in rank, Mrs Abdulrasak was posted alongside them to the North-Eastern region. Their team was led by a seasoned ambassador whose calm authority set the tone for the assignment. They were to visit several states, engage with local authorities, and represent the ministry's presence in a region marked by complexity and diversity.

For her, the assignment was more than a professional obligation. It was an opportunity to see her country through fresh eyes. She approached the journey with curiosity and gratitude, eager to learn, serve, and understand the cultural and political nuances of the states they would visit. She carried the humility of a learner and the quiet confidence of someone shaped by responsibility long before she entered the service.

When they arrived in Bauchi, the city welcomed them with a calm rhythm that contrasted with the intensity of their schedule. The team prepared for the next day's engagements, unaware that the assignment was about to shift dramatically. That evening, the head of delegation received an urgent call from headquarters. He was needed in Abuja immediately.

The atmosphere shifted as he gathered the team to inform them.

Senior officers stood around him, some concerned, others curious about what would happen next.

Then, in a moment that would alter the trajectory of her career, he turned to her.

In front of the entire team, he said, "Mrs Abdulrasaq will be representing me as I have to leave."

The words settled heavily in the room. She felt their weight immediately. She had not prepared for this. She had not imagined leadership would be handed to her so suddenly, especially in a team of officers older and more senior than she was. But leadership does not always arrive with ceremony. Sometimes it arrives abruptly, placing a mantle on your shoulders before you have time to question whether you are ready.

In that moment, she became an accidental leader, accidental only in timing, not in capacity. Life had been preparing her for years. The first-child training, the instinct to step forward, and the quiet strength she carried all rose to the surface. She accepted the responsibility with humility, aware of the eyes watching her, the expectations, and the significance of the moment.

What followed surprised her. The officers, mostly men and senior to her in age and rank, co-operated fully. They followed her lead, deferred to her decisions, and treated her with the dignity befitting the role she had been given. There was no resistance, no questioning, no undermining. Instead, there was a quiet acknowledgement that leadership had found her, and they honoured it.

From one state to another, she led the delegation with clarity and composure. She coordinated meetings, represented the ministry, engaged with local authorities, and ensured the assignment proceeded smoothly despite the unexpected change. Each day strengthened her confidence. Each successful engagement affirmed her ability. Each challenge revealed a new layer of resilience she had not known she possessed.

By the end of the assignment, she had grown in ways she could not have imagined. She had learned that leadership is not always planned; sometimes it is bestowed.

She had learned that she could rise to any occasion if she trusted her preparation. She had also learned that opportunities often come disguised as disruptions. This experience became one of the defining moments of her career, teaching her to believe in her own capacity and to give younger officers opportunities later in her career, just as she had been given one.

Visibility, Voice, and the Moment of Becoming

Years later, when Olufolake found herself in London on her first foreign posting, she carried the memory of that Nigerian assignment with her. London was a world of polished diplomacy, where nations negotiated, collaborated, and sometimes collided. The institution was larger, more formal, and more complex than anything she had encountered before. It was a system that assessed before it accepted, and observed before it trusted.

She entered this environment with humility and curiosity. She followed her colleagues to every meeting, absorbing the atmosphere of international engagement, learning the rhythms of global diplomacy, and watching seasoned officers navigate spaces where power was both visible and concealed. She understood that the institution was watching her, evaluating her, and measuring her capacity to hold authority in a room where experience, hierarchy, and gender intersected in complex ways.

One day in particular stands out in her memory. She accompanied a senior colleague to a meeting at the International Maritime Organisation. Delegates from various countries and international organisations filled the room. Flags lined the tables. The air carried the quiet tension of global deliberation. She sat quietly, taking notes, observing the proceedings, and preparing to learn from the experience.

Then, unexpectedly, the moment came.

When it was Nigeria's turn to speak, her senior colleague turned to her and said, "You will present Nigeria's position today."

She was stunned. She had not prepared for this. She hesitated, but he looked at her with calm assurance and said, "*I have faith in you.*"

Those words unlocked something within her. She took the Nigerian flag, held it firmly, and walked to the podium. As she began to speak, something remarkable happened. She felt neither fear, nor inadequacy, nor unpreparedness. Instead, she felt a deep sense of purpose, as though everything in her life had been leading to this moment.

She presented Nigeria's position with clarity and confidence. She submitted the document. She represented her country with dignity. When she finished, the room responded with recognition and applause. A young woman in a male-dominated environment had risen to the occasion. She walked out of the building that day, transformed.

Lessons Learned: The Female Diplomat as a Quiet Architect of Leadership

Her journey reveals several leadership principles that define the modern female diplomat. The institution often introduces women to leadership through disruption rather than preparation. The sudden delegation of authority in Nigeria and the unplanned visibility in London were institutional tests designed to assess Olufolake's capacity to shoulder responsibility in environments shaped by hierarchy and gendered expectations.

Legitimacy in diplomacy is earned through conduct, clarity, and institutional intelligence. Her ability to lead senior officers without resistance demonstrated that authority is not always tied to rank; it is tied to presence, steadiness, and competence.

Visibility in international spaces is often activated by leaders who intentionally extend trust. When her senior colleague asked her to speak for her country, he disrupted the institutional hesitation that often surrounds women's authority in formal settings.

Leadership is a cumulative architecture shaped by early socialisation, institutional exposure, and the courage to respond to unanticipated demands. Her childhood responsibilities, her Nigerian assignment, and her London moment formed a coherent leadership identity rooted in resilience and quiet authority.

Most importantly, the female diplomat becomes a catalyst for institutional evolution when she chooses to reproduce the opportunities she received. By extending trust to younger officers, Amb. (Prof) Olufolake Abdulrasaq widens the pathway for others and subtly reshapes the institution from within.

Her story affirms that the institution does not merely shape the female diplomat; she becomes a quiet architect of the institution's transformation.

CHAPTER FORTY-FIVE

The Cost and the Gift of Her Visibility

The Weight of Being Seen

The morning sun rose gradually over Port-au-Prince, casting a warm light across the hills as Ambassador Mireille Dufour stepped onto her balcony. The city was waking, with vendors setting up their stalls, uniformed children hurrying to school, and the hum of motorcycles weaving through narrow streets. She observed it all with quiet composure, her hands wrapped around a cup of tea, her breath steady, her mind already contemplating the day ahead.

Visibility had consistently been a paradox in her life, an element that both elevated and exposed her, strengthened and challenged her, honoured and burdened her. It was one of the most intricate aspects of her professional life. It was both a gift and a burden, a responsibility she had not entirely sought but bore with deliberate dignity.

Her visibility extended well beyond the public eye, carrying symbolic weight. It signified being the sole woman in a room where decisions influence entire continents. It entailed being scrutinised more intensely, judged more swiftly, and remembered more vividly. It embodied the expectation to excel not only for herself but also for every woman aspiring to follow.

She recognised that her mistakes would resonate more loudly than her successes.

She understood that her presence would be interpreted before her words were heard. She understood that her silence would be read as meaning, her stillness as strategy, and her composure as commentary.

However, she also acknowledged that visibility was a form of authority, the capacity to alter perceptions simply by occupying spaces once considered inaccessible to her. This ability to redefine leadership, expand representation, and embody a narrative that challenged sceptics' presumptions exemplified her influence. Her visibility served as an understated form of advocacy, expressed not through speeches but through her presence, and not through proclamations but through her conduct.

The Discipline Visibility Demands

Mireille learned early that visibility required discipline. It demanded a consistent demeanour under scrutiny and inner resilience to withstand projections, assumptions, and expectations. She had to understand that she was perceived even in silence, interpreted through stillness, and evaluated by the precision of her work.

Her visibility became a constant mirror, reflecting not only her actions but also the world's biases.

She remembered her first major multilateral meeting in Geneva. She had walked into the room with her briefing notes neatly arranged, her arguments prepared, and her confidence steady. Yet before she spoke a single word, she felt the weight of eyes on her, assessing, questioning, measuring. She was the only

Black woman in the room. The only Caribbean diplomat at the table. The only person whose presence disrupted the unspoken uniformity of the space.

She had felt the familiar tightening in her chest, the quiet pressure to prove, justify, and validate her presence. But she had also felt something else: a rising clarity. She was not there to blend in. She was there to represent truth. She was there to embody possibility. She was there to shift the room simply by being in it.

Visibility demanded that she hold herself with intention.
Visibility demanded that she speak with precision.
Visibility demanded that she carry herself with a dignity that could withstand misinterpretation.

Yet visibility also gave her a vantage point. It allowed her to observe the machinery of global power from within. It revealed the fragility of systems that seemed unshakeable from the outside. It showed her how influence was cultivated, how alliances were formed, and how narratives were constructed.

Her visibility granted her access not only to rooms but also to insight.

The Truth She Learns About Being Seen

Over time, Mireille realised that the cost of visibility was not exhaustion; it was exposure. Exposure to scrutiny. Exposure to expectation. Exposure to the world's projections, both generous and cruel.

But the gift of visibility was not recognition; it was impact.

She learned that she could not control how the world saw her, but she could control what she stood for. She could not control the expectations placed upon her, but she could uphold the integrity with which she met them. She could not control the narratives written about her, but she could hold fast to the truth she carried within.

She remembered a moment during her posting in Nairobi, when a young intern approached her after a panel discussion. The intern's voice trembled as she said, "I've never seen someone who looks like me speak the way you did. You made me believe I could be here too."

Mireille smiled, but inside she felt something shift, a recognition that her visibility was not merely personal. It was generational. It was communal. It was a bridge between what had been and what could be.

Her visibility evolved into a form of leadership. It signalled to those watching from afar. It reassured those uncertain of their place in the world. It quietly invited those who had not yet found the courage to step forward.

She recognised that her presence in these spaces was deliberate, necessary, and meaningful.

The Private Cost Behind the Public Composure

Yet visibility was not without its private cost. There were nights when she returned to her hotel room after a long day of meetings, feeling the weight of being seen settle into her bones. There were moments when she longed for anonymity, for the freedom to be imperfect without consequence, for the luxury of being ordinary.

She remembered one evening in Brussels, when she sat alone in her room, the city lights flickering outside her window. She had just delivered a statement that drew both praise and criticism.

Her inbox was full of messages, some supportive, some harsh, some questioning her competence, motives, and right to speak. She closed her laptop, leaned back in her chair, and allowed herself a moment of vulnerability. She felt the ache of exposure, the ache of being visible in a world that scrutinised her more than others, expected more of her, and demanded more. But she also felt something else, something deeper, steadier, more enduring.

She felt purpose.
She felt alignment.
She felt the truth.

Visibility was not easy.
But it was meaningful.
And meaning, she knew, was worth the cost.

The Interwoven Cost and Gift

Ultimately, Mireille understood that the costs and gifts of her visibility were inseparable. The costs refined her, while the gifts expanded her. The visibility that once felt burdensome became the very instrument through which she established a legacy that outlasted her tenure. She became visible not because she sought the spotlight, but because she carried a light the world could no longer ignore.

Her visibility was not a performance.
It was a presence.
It was not a burden.
It was a calling.
It was not a spotlight.
It was a signal to every woman watching, waiting, wondering whether she belonged.

Mireille understood that she was not visible for herself alone.
She was visible to the women who had come before her.
She was visible to the women who would come after her.
She was visible to the women who had been silenced, overlooked, underestimated, or erased.

Her visibility was a testament, not to her perfection, but to her perseverance.

Lesson Learnt

Mireille learns that the cost of visibility is exposure, yet its gift is impact. She discovers that she cannot control how the world sees her, but she can control what she stands for. She realises that visibility is not a burden but a calling, a quiet form of leadership that reshapes rooms simply by being present. And she understands that the woman who becomes visible does not seek the spotlight; she becomes the light the world can no longer ignore.

CHAPTER FORTY-SIX

The Future of Women in Diplomacy

The Future That Will Not Be Left to Chance

The dawn of the desert gently illuminated Amman, casting a subdued golden hue upon the city's limestone edifices. Economic Attaché Ms Samira El-Badawi stood at her office window, observing the sunrise over the surrounding hills. The environment was tranquil, suspended in a delicate stillness before activity. She perceived the significance of the moment, not as a burden but as an opening for opportunity.

The progression of women in diplomatic roles would not occur by mere chance. It would be intentionally crafted through institutional policies, the courage demonstrated by women within decision-making spaces, and the increasing international acknowledgement of their contributions. The upcoming generation of female diplomats would inherit a landscape reshaped by their predecessors, although it would still bear traces of former structures that once limited their forerunners.

Ms El-Badawi comprehended this profoundly. She embarked on her diplomatic career during a period when women were present but not yet wholly integrated into the framework of influence. She observed senior female diplomats navigate environments not originally designed for their participation, systems not constructed with their inclusion in mind, and expectations moulded by assumptions they did not formulate.

The future, she knew, would demand something different.

Not assimilation.

Not endurance.

Not quite excellence.

But reimagination.

The next generation of women would not be asked to fit into the old framework. They would be asked to redesign it.

The Leadership the Future Demands

Samira's work as an economic attaché had taught her that the world was shifting rapidly, unpredictably, and irreversibly. Markets were volatile. Alliances remained fluid. Crises revealed interconnectedness. Power was no longer concentrated in predictable centres. Diplomacy extended beyond traditional statecraft; it encompassed economic resilience, technological adaptation, environmental sustainability, and human dignity.

The future demanded a different style of leadership, one grounded in depth rather than dominance, perception rather than performance, and humanity rather than hierarchy. Women would not merely occupy diplomatic positions; they would redefine their purpose. They would bring a form of intelligence that was analytical and intuitive, strategic and empathetic, firm and adaptable. Their leadership would transcend imitation of past paradigms and evolve beyond them.

Samira had observed this evolution begin. She had witnessed young women entering the diplomatic service with a fluency in complexity that seemed almost instinctive. They understood that diplomacy was no longer a linear endeavour.

They understood that influence was no longer loud. They understood that leadership was no longer about command, but about coherence.

The world they would inherit would be more complex than the one their predecessors navigated.
Crises would be more interconnected.
Conflicts are more diffuse.
Power is more fragmented.

Diplomacy would require the ability to interpret not only the explicit content of negotiations but also the emotional and psychological subtext that shaped them. Women might be uniquely prepared for this, not because of inherent superiority, but because history has compelled them to understand complexity to survive.

The Structural Shift

Samira knew that the future of diplomacy would depend on the capacity to build trust across divides, to preserve nuance in environments that rewarded simplicity, and to sustain dialogue when silence felt easier. Women would contribute to this future through leadership forged in resilience, refined by exclusion, and strengthened by navigating systems not originally designed for them.

But she also knew that individual brilliance was not enough. Institutions had to evolve.

Systems had to begin to acknowledge the cost of emotional labour, value diverse perspectives, and create environments where women did not merely endure but thrived. This shift would move from tokenism to transformation, from representation to redistribution, from inclusion as a gesture to inclusion as governance.

She had seen the early signs of this shift: mentorship programs, gender-balanced panels, flexible work structures, and leadership pipelines. But she also knew that these were beginnings, not conclusions. The future required more than symbolic gestures. It required structural redesign.

Women could not be expected to thrive in systems that had never been built with them in mind.

The systems themselves had to change.

The Women Who Build New Tables

Samira often thought of the young women she mentored, brilliant, determined, unafraid. They were not waiting for permission to lead. They were not waiting for validation. They were not waiting for the world to recognise their worth. They were preparing to build new tables.

She had seen them challenge outdated assumptions with quiet confidence. She had seen them propose solutions that blended innovation with empathy. She had seen them refuse to shrink themselves to fit into rooms too small for their vision. Their success would not be measured by conformity to existing norms, but by their courage to reshape them.

As they rose, they would carry the lessons of their predecessors, women who stood alone in rooms of power, who negotiated without recognition, and who held nations together in silence. The future would not erase their struggles; it would honour them by ensuring no woman had to fight the same battles again.

Samira often thought of her grandmother, a woman who had never left Jordan, never stepped into a diplomatic room, yet had taught her the essence of leadership: clarity, dignity, and courage. She carried her grandmother's lessons into every negotiation, every meeting, every decision.

The next generation would carry the lessons of women like her, women who had paved the way not through visibility but through endurance.

The Inevitability of Their Influence

One evening, as Samira walked through the quiet corridors of the embassy, she paused before a framed photograph of the first woman to serve in her country's foreign ministry. Their faces were solemn, dignified, and resolute. They had entered the service at a time when their presence was questioned, their competence doubted, and their ambitions dismissed.

Yet they had persisted. And because they had persisted, she was here.

She realised then that the future of women in diplomacy was not a question. It was an inevitability. It was the unfolding of a truth that generations had laboured to articulate: that the world was wiser, stronger, and more just when women shaped its direction.

The future would not be perfect.
But it would be different.
And it would be different because women would make it so.

Lessons Learnt

She learns that the future of women in diplomacy is not a possibility but a certainty. She discovers that leadership will evolve not by imitation but by reimagination. She realises that institutions must transform if women are to thrive, and that the next generation will not wait for permission to lead. And she understands that the influence of women in diplomacy is not emerging; it is inevitable.

CHAPTER FORTY-SEVEN

The Unseen Forces That Shape Nations

The Power Beneath the Surface

The late-afternoon sun cast long shadows across Nairobi's government quarter as Senior Policy Analyst Kezia Mwangi walked at a measured pace towards her office. The corridors were quiet, and the day's usual bustle gradually gave way to the evening's quietude. She paused by the window, taking in the city, a metropolis vibrant with movement, ambition, contradictions, and hope. From this vantage point, she observed the tangible mechanics of national life: vehicles manoeuvring through roundabouts, citizens hurrying home, and lights flickering across the skyline.

Yet she knew the true forces shaping the nation were not visible from any window.

Treaties, elections, or official declarations do not solely mould nations. They are shaped by forces that rarely appear in official documents, operating quietly beneath the surface of public consciousness. Kezia had come to recognise these forces not through abstract theory but through lived experience. She had realised that the world is governed as much by the unspoken as by the written, as much by the invisible as by the visible, and as much by the emotional ambience of a room as by the legal texts before her.

She understood that the most pivotal shifts in a nation's trajectory often originate in silence, in the moments before a leader speaks, in the hesitation preceding a decision, in the subtle tension that pervades a room when truth confronts diplomacy.

The Human Psychology Behind Global Decisions

Kezia's work had taken her into rooms where the stakes were high and the emotions even higher. She had watched leaders speak with confidence while concealing fear. She had seen negotiators argue passionately while masking uncertainty. She had observed how pride shaped decisions more than data, how memory influenced policy more than logic, and how history lingered in the air long after documents were signed.

She came to understand that nations were shaped by the temperament of their leaders, by the fears they concealed, the ambitions they nurtured, and the insecurities they refused to acknowledge. She learned that global decisions were influenced not only by logic but also by memory, pride, history, and the unresolved wounds that lingered between states.

She observed how a single sentence could alter an alliance, how a solitary gesture could soften a hardened stance, and how a single silence could change the course of a negotiation.

She remembered one meeting vividly, a tense regional consultation in which two delegations sat opposite each other, their histories heavy in the room. The conversation was polite, the language diplomatic, yet the air was thick with unspoken grievances. It was not the words exchanged that shifted the meeting; it was the moment when one delegate laid down his pen, exhaled, and allowed vulnerability to soften his posture. That single gesture opened a door no argument had been able to unlock.

It was then that Kezia realised: Nations move not only through policy but through psychology.

The Diplomacy That Happens Between the Lines

Over time, she recognised that diplomacy went beyond merely managing interests; it required interpreting underlying currents. It meant identifying unspoken sentiments, analysing the emotional dynamics in a room, and understanding the psychological landscape behind a counterpart's stance.

She learned to listen not only to explicit statements but also to what was deliberately avoided.
She became adept at observing not only the arguments presented but also the emotions beneath them.
She learned to sense not only the direction of negotiations but also the energy that shaped them.

She understood that nations are influenced by the private uncertainties of public figures, discreet calculations made in corridors, and the trust built in moments not recorded in official records.

She recalled walking down a quiet corridor after a long meeting, overhearing two senior officials speaking in hushed tones, not about strategy but about fear. Fear of miscalculation. Fear of public backlash. Fear of losing face. Fear of being misunderstood. That whispered conversation, spoken in exhaustion, revealed more about the negotiation's future than anything said during the formal session.

Diplomacy, she realised, transpired between the lines, within the pauses, the glances, the hesitations, and the subtle shifts in tone.

The Invisible Foundations of Power

Kezia recognised that the intangible forces shaping nations included the resilience of communities, the dignity of individuals who endured adversity without recognition, the cultural memory that guided societal decisions, and the collective aspirations that transcended political cycles.

These forces were not recorded in policy briefs, yet they determined the success or failure of policies. They were not debated in plenary halls, yet they influenced every vote cast there.

She learned that a nation’s strength was not measured solely by its military capabilities or economic prosperity, but by the coherence of its identity, the stability of its institutions, and the trust its people placed in their leaders.

She knew that the most significant shifts in international relations often occurred long before they became visible, in the erosion of trust, the intensification of grievances, and the quiet accumulation of unmet needs.

She remembered visiting a rural community during a research assignment. The people spoke not of geopolitics, but of dignity, the dignity of being heard, the dignity of being seen, and the dignity of being valued. She realised then that national stability was rooted not in grand strategies, but in the quiet strength of ordinary people.

The Moment She Realises She Is One of These Forces

One evening, after a particularly intense policy review, Kezia sat alone in her office, the city lights shimmering below. She felt the day's weight settle on her shoulders, the decisions made, the tensions navigated, the truths spoken and unspoken.

And then she realised something she had never fully acknowledged: she herself had become one of the unseen forces shaping her nation.

Her presence altered the dynamic of a room.
Her clarity shaped the tone.
Her integrity shaped the outcome.

She had become part of the invisible architecture that sustained national stability, not through spectacle but through consistency; not through dominance but through discernment; not through force but through the quiet authority of a perceptive mind that saw beyond the surface.

She realised that her work would never be fully visible, never fully recognised, never fully understood. But it would matter. It would endure. It would shape the nation in ways no headline could capture.

The Work That Endures Beyond Her Tenure

Ultimately, Kezia understood that nations were shaped not only by power, but by wisdom. They were shaped by the courage to face difficult truths, the humility to listen, and the discipline to act with foresight rather than impulse.

She knew her responsibility was to uphold these principles, ensuring that the unseen foundations of peace, justice, and dignity remained intact even amid upheaval.

This was the work that endured.
This was the work that outlasted her tenure.
This was the work that shaped nations long after the headlines faded.

CHAPTER FORTY-EIGHT

The Summoning of the Next Generation

The Inheritance They Did Not Choose but Must Carry

The evening illumination of Singapore reflected across Marina Bay as Cultural Affairs Officer Liyun Zhang stood on the rooftop terrace of her ministry building. The cityscape below was vibrant, efficient, contemporary, and forward-looking, yet she sensed the influence of something ancient, an inheritance far greater than the skyline before her. Each successive generation of diplomats inherits a world shaped by their predecessors' decisions.

However, the next generation of women entering diplomacy will inherit more: a legacy shaped by silence, resilience, courage, and the unwavering efforts of women who occupied roles not originally intended for them. Liyun often reflected on these women, those who entered rooms where their presence was questioned, participated in meetings where their voices were undervalued, and bore the weight of nations without recognition.

Their sacrifices may not always have been documented, but their impact remains unmistakable. The call to the next generation is not merely ceremonial; it is a summons to progress with clarity, to lead with integrity, and to carry forward the unfinished work.

The World That Will Demand Their Depth

The world awaiting them would not be gentle. It would be complex, volatile, and impatient. It would demand a depth of discernment that could not be taught in classrooms, a stability that could not be borrowed, and a courage that could not be outsourced.

Liyun had already glimpsed this world in the rapid shifts of global markets, in the cultural tensions simmering beneath diplomatic pleasantries, and in the technological disruptions that reshaped alliances overnight. She knew the next generation of women would be asked to manage crises without precedent, mediate conflicts rooted in histories beyond their borders, and articulate the truth in environments where honesty was inconvenient.

They would be summoned not because they felt ready, but because the world would need them before they were.

She remembered her first multilateral forum, a gathering of young diplomats from across Asia. The discussions were intense, the stakes high, the pace relentless. She had felt unprepared, overwhelmed, and out of her depth. But she had also felt something else: a growing clarity that the world was shifting faster than institutions could adapt, and that her generation would be asked to bridge that gap.

The Discipline and Posture They Must Cultivate

They must understand that diplomacy is more than a profession. It was a discipline of the mind and a posture of the spirit. It required listening beyond words, seeing beyond appearances, and contemplating beyond borders.

Liyun had learned this slowly, through moments that tested her patience, challenged her assumptions, and stretched her capacity for empathy. She had learned that diplomacy demanded unwavering commitment to justice, resilience in the face of cynicism, and fidelity to truth, even when truth was costly.

For the next generation, leadership would not be the pursuit of visibility but the cultivation of vision. Not the accumulation of influence but the stewardship of responsibility. Not the demonstration of strength but the practice of coherence. She had already seen young women in her ministry embody this: interns who asked bold questions, junior officers who challenged outdated norms, and analysts who brought nuance to discussions long oversimplified. They were not waiting for permission to think deeply. They were already doing it.

The Lineage They Join

These future leaders would be called not to power, but to an understanding of its implications. They would not walk alone. They would walk on foundations laid by women who negotiated without recognition, endured without acknowledgement, and stood alone so others would not have to.

Liyun often thought of her mentor, a retired diplomat who had served when women were rare in the foreign service. She had once told Liyun, "We walked so you could run. But you must run so others can fly."

Those words stayed with her.

The next generation would inherit not only the spaces these women entered but also the courage that enabled them to remain. Their task was not to imitate the past but to honour it by building a future in which no woman's presence was questioned, no woman's voice dismissed, and no woman's leadership regarded as extraordinary.

They would inherit a lineage of women who had carried nations in silence, held institutions together through sheer resilience, and shaped global outcomes without ever being named in official histories.

The Testing and the Revelation

Diplomacy would test them. It would stretch their patience, challenge their convictions, and confront them with moments when the cost of integrity felt unbearably high.

Liyun had already experienced this testing. She remembered a cultural negotiation that had taken months, a delicate dialogue between two countries with a long history of misunderstanding. She had been the youngest officer in the room, yet the responsibility placed on her felt immense. There were moments when she questioned her capacity, when the weight of expectation pressed on her chest.

But diplomacy had also revealed her strength.
It had sharpened her wisdom.
It had offered her the profound privilege of shaping the world not by force but by clarity.

She knew the next generation would face similar moments, when they would be summoned to lead with steadiness amid uncertainty, with dignity amid provocation, and with courage amid isolation. Moments when they would be asked to carry nations without losing themselves, to navigate power without being hardened by it, and to remain human in systems that often forgot humanity.

The Invitation They Must Accept

Ultimately, the summoning of the next generation was not a directive. It was an invitation to join a lineage of women who transformed diplomacy not by imitating the world they encountered, but by elevating it.

It was an invitation to ascend, with the understanding that the world they inherited was flawed, yet the world they could shape might be fundamentally different.

Liyun looked out over the city, a city that had risen from limited land and vast ambition, embodying the possibility of transformation. She felt the weight of the future, but also its promise.

This was their moment.
This was their mantle.
This was their summoning.

CHAPTER FORTY-NINE

When Silence Speaks

The Power She Learns to Wield Without Words

The evening call to prayer drifted softly across Manama as Deputy Consul General Farah Al-Hashimi sat alone in her office, the city lights shimmering through the glass. The day had been long, with meetings steeped in tension, negotiations threaded with unspoken truths, and conversations heavy with what could not be said aloud. Yet in the quiet of her office, something settled within her, something she had learned only through years of navigating the delicate terrain of diplomacy.

There came a moment in the life of a female diplomat when she realised that not every truth required articulation. Some truths spoke more powerfully through presence, restraint, or silence.

Silence became more than the absence of speech.

It became a form of profound understanding, a clarity so deep that words would only dilute it.

Farah discovered that silence was not weakness, not surrender, not retreat. Silence was power.

It was a power that did not announce itself, seek validation, or depend on volume. It was the power of a woman who had seen enough, learned enough, and become enough to know that not every battle was fought aloud.

The Silence That Shapes the Room

Farah learned that silence could shape a room more decisively than argument. She had seen it in tense bilateral meetings, in multilateral forums, and in private consultations where the stakes were high and the emotions even higher.

Silence became the space in which she gathered herself, listened for what others could not hear, and discerned the difference between urgency and noise.

She remembered one negotiation vividly. Two delegations sat across from each other, their positions rigid, their tones sharp. Voices rose, tempers flared, and the room seemed on the verge of collapse. Farah remained silent, not out of fear but out of discipline. She watched, listened, and observed the emotional undercurrents shaping the conversation.

And then, when the moment was right, she spoke, one sentence, measured and precise. The room shifted. The tension eased. The conversation recalibrated.

Then she understood:
Silence is not the absence of influence.
It is the preparation for it.

Silence unsettled those who relied on dominance.
Silence steadied those who depended on her presence.
Silence revealed truths that rhetoric sought to obscure.

Silence became her instrument, precise, intentional, rooted in discipline. She used it not to withdraw from the world, but to engage with it more wisely.

The Silence That Protects Her

Farah also recognised that silence could be a form of protection. It shielded her from the exhaustion of constant explanation. It guarded her against the temptation to justify her existence. It protected her from the emotional erosion that accompanied perpetual visibility.

She had learned early in her career that women were often expected to explain themselves, their decisions, their presence, and their competence. She had learned that silence could disrupt that expectation. It could create boundaries where none had been offered. It could preserve her integrity in a world that continually sought to fragment her.

She remembered a moment from her first posting when a senior colleague questioned her judgment in a meeting. The room fell silent, waiting for her to defend herself. Instead, she looked at him, steady, calm, unshaken. Her silence unsettled him more than any argument could. It revealed his insecurity, not her inadequacy.

Silence became her shield, not to hide behind, but to stand within.

The Silence That Reveals Others

But silence was not only a protection.

It was a revelation.

Silence revealed who listened.
Silence revealed who understood.
Silence revealed who underestimated her.
Silence revealed who feared the clarity she carried.

In silence, she saw the true architecture of power, who rushed to fill the void, who grew uneasy, who grew attentive, who grew sincere. Silence became a mirror in which the world laid itself bare.

Farah learned to watch how people responded to silence. Some grew anxious, mistaking it for disapproval. Some grew defensive, projecting their insecurities onto her stillness. Some grew thoughtful, recognising the invitation to reflect. And some grew respectful, understanding that silence was not emptiness but depth.

Silence taught her more about people than their words ever could.

The Silence That Refines Her Voice

Yet silence was not the end of her voice.

It was its refinement.

Silence taught her to speak only when her words could shift something essential. Through maturity, she learned that not every moment required intervention, not every provocation deserved a response, and not every injustice demanded an immediate reaction. She learned that speaking on impulse diluted her power, whereas speaking with clarity amplified it.

Silence taught her to choose her battles with discernment, to conserve her strength for moments of consequence, and to speak only when it served a purpose rather than ego.

She remembered a moment when a junior colleague asked her, “How do you know when to speak?” Farah smiled gently and replied, “When silence has done all it can.”

The Silence That Becomes Her Legacy

In the final phase of her journey, Farah came to understand that silence was not merely emptiness. Rather, it signified fullness, the fullness of a life lived with purpose, the richness of lessons earned through adversity, and the profundity of wisdom moulded by experience.

Silcncc became the language of a woman who no longer felt compelled to prove anything, neither to the world, nor to institutions, nor even to herself.

When silence arrived, it carried the weight of all her lived experience. It conveyed the authority of every room she entered, every truth she upheld, and every decision she made. It communicated with the clarity of a woman who understood that her true power had never resided in her volume, but in her presence.

Ultimately, silence became her final gift, neither as withdrawal nor as avoidance, but as a manifestation of wisdom; not as an absence, but as a legacy. It became the space she fostered for others to ascend, the space she created for the next generation to voice their perspectives, and the space where her diplomatic journey concluded, and theirs commenced.

Because when silence speaks, it does not terminate the dialogue. Instead, it initiates a new one.

And the world listens attentively.

CHAPTER FIFTY

The Enduring Architecture of Her Legacy

The Corridor of a Lifetime

The corridor was long, quiet, and dimly lit, the kind that held memory in its walls. Permanent Secretary Amina Diallo traversed it at a deliberate pace, her footsteps softly resonating on the polished flooring. It marked her concluding evening within the Ministry, to which she had dedicated thirty-five years of service, and the surrounding silence imparted a sense of reverence.

She moved with the composure of one who had silently borne her nation's responsibilities, the dignity of an individual committed to public service, and the humility of one who recognised that her legacy was not merely the echo of her name, but the structural framework she had established. As she proceeded, the corridor seemed to breathe alongside her, each step awakening memories she had not actively invoked, yet which emerged gently, like truths returning to their source.

The First Unseen Victory

She remembered her first posting, decades earlier, when she was a young Second Secretary in Addis Ababa. She had been twenty-seven, earnest and observant, still learning the unspoken language of diplomacy. In a crowded conference room, delegates argued over a draft communiqué, their voices sharp, tempers rising.

A single mistranslated phrase had shifted the meaning of a paragraph, turning a neutral statement into an accusation. No one noticed. No one except her. She leaned towards her ambassador and whispered the correction, her voice steady despite her pounding heart.

The meeting paused. The error was corrected, and the tension dissolved. No one applauded her. No one recorded her intervention. No one remembered her name. But she remembered the truth: she had saved her country from a crisis before it began. It was the first time she understood that the most important work a diplomat does is often unseen.

The Night She Protected Her Nation

She continued walking, and another memory rose, heavier, older, shaped by the weight of experience. She was now in Ottawa, a mid-career Counsellor, navigating a bilateral misunderstanding that threatened to escalate. A foreign official had made a statement that was misinterpreted back home, and the draft response prepared by her delegation was reactive, emotional, and dangerously sharp. She had read it at midnight, alone in her office, the glow of her desk lamp illuminating the words that could damage years of trust. She stayed through the night, rewriting the statement line by line, transforming it into something measured, dignified, and steady.

At dawn, she presented it to her ambassador, who questioned the delay, her edits, and her judgment. She absorbed the criticism quietly, without defending herself. Hours later, the revised statement was released and praised internationally for its restraint.

It de-escalated the tension and preserved the relationship. No one knew she had written it. No one thanked her. No one remembered her sacrifice. But she remembered. And God remembered.

The Silence That Saved a Region

The corridor narrowed slightly as she approached the final stretch, and the third memory rose, the one that had shaped her most deeply. She was Director of Regional Affairs then, seated at a multilateral meeting that had spiralled into hostility. Delegates argued, accusations flew, and the air was thick with old grievances.

A rupture was imminent, one that could destabilise regional cooperation for years. She remembered watching the room carefully, sensing the emotional temperature rise like heat beneath a closed door. And then she did something no one expected.

She said nothing.

She let the silence expand, not as absence but as intervention.

The room grew uneasy.

The noise softened.

The tension paused. And in that silence, she spoke one sentence: “Let us not destroy in one hour what took us decades to build.” The room shifted. The anger deflated. The meeting recalibrated. The rupture was avoided.

The region was steadied. The future was protected. No one recorded her sentence in the minutes. No one credited her with the turning point. No one acknowledged the wisdom she carried. But she knew. And the region she saved would never know how close it came to breaking.

The Realisation at the End of the Corridor

She reached the end of the corridor and paused, her hand resting on the cool metal handle of the exit door. Behind her lay thirty-five years of service, years of unseen labour, unrecorded victories, and unspoken sacrifices. Ahead of her lay a life she had not yet lived. In that stillness, she understood something profound: her legacy was not in the applause she never received, nor in the speeches she never gave, nor in the titles she earned.

Her legacy was in the architecture she built, the stability she preserved, the crises she prevented, the dignity she protected, the wisdom she embodied, the clarity she carried, the truth she upheld, and the humanity she refused to lose.

Her legacy lived in the people she mentored, the officers she steadied, and the young women who watched her and believed they could rise.

Her legacy lived in the atmosphere she created, a quiet current that shifted the tone of rooms, a silent strength that shaped decisions, and a steady presence that held the ministry together. Her legacy lived in the God she served, not in words but in discipline, humility, and integrity. Her legacy lived in the nation she loved, not in grand gestures but in unseen sacrifices, unrecorded victories, and the quiet architecture of her character.

The Final Offering

She stepped outside. The night air embraced her, warm and familiar. The stars above Dakar shimmered like witnesses. She whispered a prayer, not for herself but for the nation. For every officer who would rise after her. For every woman who would walk these halls. For every truth that must be upheld. For every decision that must be made with clarity. For every legacy that must continue.

She did not look back.

She did not need to.

Her journey concluded.

Her influence continued.

Her legacy stood. And the architecture she built, quiet, steady, unshakeable, would hold long after her name faded from memory because she had lived with intention. Because she had served with humility. Because she had given her life to God and the nation.

This was her final offering.

This was her enduring architecture.

This was her legacy.

She finally understood that her greatest diplomacy was the quiet architecture of the woman she had become, a truth that settled over her like evening light. As the night embraced her, the world shifted gently, recognising the depth of a life lived with intention. She walked forward, not diminished but complete, a woman who had mastered herself.

Afterword

The trajectory of the female diplomat's career is not straightforward. It follows a cyclical pattern of ascension, perseverance, disruption, reconstruction, and self-renewal. As global circumstances evolve, the expectations placed upon her will adapt. Nonetheless, the fundamental objectives of her role endure: to foster avenues for peace in a world often inclined towards conflict, to articulate truth within systems that favour ambiguity, and to exemplify dignity in challenging environments.

This book concludes, but her story does not. It continues in every woman who steps into the arena with clarity, courage, and conviction, women who carry nations in their hearts, negotiate in silence, and stand with integrity even when unseen. The female diplomat's journey is never truly finished. It lives on in the legacy she leaves, the spaces she transforms, and the future she quietly shapes.

Acknowledgments

This book was shaped by the women who entrusted me with their stories, by colleagues who demonstrated dignity in challenging environments, by mentors who believed in the quiet strength of presence, and by the communities that supported me across continents.

I am grateful to every diplomat who has previously traversed this path, to every young woman preparing to follow it, and to my family, whose love has served as my unwavering anchor during each posting.

Above all, I acknowledge the grace that has sustained me through seasons of silence, seasons of courage, and seasons of transformation.

Acknowledgement of the Next Generation

To the women who will read this book and recognise fragments of themselves within its pages, this work is dedicated to you. You who enter spaces not designed with you in mind, yet do so with a steadiness that challenges the established order. You who convey nations through your voice, posture, silence, and discernment. You who negotiate not only across borders but also within yourselves, balancing duty with identity, ambition with integrity, and visibility with safety.

May you rise with clarity.

May you lead with conviction.

May you refuse to diminish yourself for the sake of others' comfort.

May you remember that your presence in any room is already an act of disrupting history.

The world you inherit is imperfect, fractured by conflict, shaped by inequity, and sustained by systems that often neglect the women who uphold them. Yet the world you will shape will differ because you enter it consciously, understanding that leadership is not performance but presence, not dominance but discernment.

Not noise, but alignment.

May you never apologise for your strength.

May you never compromise your worth.

May you never forget that your voice is a diplomatic instrument, capable of transforming atmospheres, alleviating tensions, and fostering new opportunities. And when the workload becomes burdensome, as it inevitably will, may you return to yourself with tenderness.

May you find peace in your own transformation. May you remember that you are not solitary; you stand within a lineage of women who have quietly, fiercely, and gracefully carried nations, often unrecognised by the world.

This book concludes, but your journey is only commencing.

Walk forward with courage.

The world awaits the diplomat you are becoming.

Note on Originality

This manuscript contains no citations. The Female Diplomat is an entirely original work, grounded in lived experience, professional observation, and the author's intellectual and emotional journey through diplomacy. While the themes intersect with broader conversations about leadership, gender, governance, diplomacy, and institutional life, the reflections presented here are not derived from external texts.

The insights, frameworks, and narratives arise from years of service, contemplation, and personal evolution in the diplomatic arena. This book stands as an independent contribution to the discourse on women in diplomacy, shaped not by academic referencing but by the author's direct engagement with the world she writes about.

About the Author

Oluwakemi T. Amuda is a distinguished career diplomat whose professional endeavours span continents, diverse cultures, and prominent international institutions, shaping her distinctive perspective on leadership, identity, and the lived experiences of women in diplomacy. With over twenty years of service, she has represented her nation with unwavering integrity, intellectual rigour, and a deep commitment to diplomacy's transformative potential. Her career across various regions has made her a voice characterised by clarity, courage, and spiritual depth in international leadership.

In addition to her professional achievements, she specialises in global leadership and strategic communications. Her literary works explore the inner dimensions of leadership: its discipline, solitude, quiet strength, and human cost. As the author of *"The Diplomatic Leader"* and "*The Fragrance,"* she is renowned for blending insight, narrative, and spiritual sensitivity into writings that resonate across professional and personal domains. "The Female Diplomat" continues this tradition, offering a rare and intimate perspective on women who serve their nations on the global stage.

She is dedicated to shaping discussions around diplomacy, women's leadership, and the evolving requirements of global service. Her writing addresses the core of leadership, the unseen struggles, the quiet victories, and the spiritual grounding necessary to hold positions of influence. Her works embody a profound belief in purpose, integrity, and the transformative potential of voice. She writes from a foundation of lived experience, intellectual rigour, and profound respect for the unseen aspects of leadership and the labour of those who stand where nations converge.

Oluwakemi's voice is both authoritative and tender, shaped by years of service, study, and spiritual stewardship. She writes not merely to inform but to awaken and empower, offering her readers a pathway to deeper understanding, resilience, and purpose in their own journeys. She illuminates the realities of diplomatic life and inspires a new generation to lead with wisdom, authenticity, and grace.

About The Book

The Female Diplomat is a profound exploration of the inner and outer worlds of women who serve as diplomats, standing at the intersection of power, purpose, and identity. It reveals the unseen dimensions of diplomacy: the emotional intelligence, spiritual resilience, and moral courage required to represent a nation while preserving one's authentic voice.

Through vivid narratives and reflective insight, the book explores the heart of global service, where ambition intersects with sacrifice and leadership is judged not only by policy but also by the quiet strength of character. It articulates the delicate balance between professional duty and personal conviction, showing how women navigate complex negotiations, cultural expectations, and the unseen burden of history. It also highlights the challenges, triumphs, and sacrifices of female diplomats on the international stage.

Beyond the corridors of embassies and conference halls, The Female Diplomat honours the humanity behind the title. It celebrates the grace, intellect, and spiritual depth of women who build bridges across nations and generations. Each page invites readers to see diplomacy not merely as a career but as a calling, a sacred stewardship of influence, empathy, and transformation. This work is both analytical and inspirational, blending lived experience with scholarly reflection. It adds a new voice to the global leadership literature, one that speaks with authority, authenticity, and divine insight into what it means to lead with power and purpose.

www.ingramcontent.com/pod-product-compliance
Lightning Source LLC
LaVergne TN
LVHW081401110826
845149LV00010B/1631